The Kitchen Book

The Kitchen Book

THE ESSENTIAL RESOURCE
FOR CREATING THE ROOM
OF YOUR DREAMS

EDITED BY BILL PARTSCH

Woman's Day Special Interest Publications

Copyright © 2007 Filipacchi Publishing USA, Inc.

First published in 2005 in the United States of America by
Filipacchi Publishing
1633 Broadway
New York, NY 10019

Woman's Day Specials and *Woman's Day Special Interest Publications*
are registered trademarks of Hachette Filipacchi Media U.S., Inc.

Design: Patricia Fabricant
Proofreading: Judith M. Gee

ISBN: 1-933231-31-9

Printed in China

Contents

Introduction

WHEN YOU THINK ABOUT IT (which I confess I do on a daily basis, as the editor of Woman's Day Special Interest Publications' *Kitchens & Baths* magazine) there's no other room in the house that's used for so many different purposes as the kitchen. Bedrooms are sleeping spaces, hygienic needs are fulfilled in the bath, home offices and media rooms are each task-specific—but kitchens are the locus for not only cooking, but eating and socializing, as well.

Kitchens have, to a large extent, claimed the functions of both the dining and living rooms. How to explain this migration? I think technology has a lot to do with it. With advances in refrigeration and freezing, cooking and cleanup methods, the entire meal-making process has become incredibly streamlined compared to the good old days of the ice man and the fruit cellar. Storing and preparing food requires less space, time, energy and effort than ever before. Stoking the fire has been replaced by pushing a button or twisting a knob; actual cooking time has decreased so precipitously that we now measure it in seconds. "Doing the dishes" has essentially become a euphemism for loading plates into the machine that washes them; the hands-on meaning of the phrase has been rendered archaic.

With the business of cooking so simplified, the kitchen has been freed to evolve from a dedicated culinary prep place to a room where other activities are welcome. The erstwhile work table was the focus of this transformation. Originally the spot to serve casual meals to immediate family, it first became a comfortable location for neighbors to sit when dropping by for a cup of coffee, and then stepped up to provide the grandstand seating for guests at dinner parties and holiday gatherings. When the table graduated in significance and centrality to become the fully featured island, replete with sinks and appliances, the kitchen achieved a prime facet of its modern identity.

When we were developing the content of this book, we considered a number of different ways to present these kitchens—as a portfolio of various styles, or sorted according to square footage, or as a regional overview. Ultimately, none of these approaches made as much sense as what we settled on: three sections devoted to spaces for cooking, for family living and for entertaining. More than decor or dimensions, what really matters is how people use their kitchens.

If trophy ranges, built-in coffeemakers and other gourmet gadgetry are the stuff that inspire your dreams, you'll enjoy looking at the kitchens for cooks. For those who need an efficient and inviting kitchen to make feeding the brood more ideal than ordeal, the pages devoted to family kitchens are for you. And with their carefully crafted floor plans and dining areas, the kitchens for entertaining are sure to appeal to frequent and occasional hosts alike.

In addition, there's an informative chapter, "What You Need to Know About...," where you'll find tips on how to select everything from counter surfacing to major appliances when planning your new kitchen.

Leslie Clagett
Editor, *Kitchens & Baths*

Design Talk

What are the essential features of a kitchen?
A kitchen must look beautiful and cook beautifully, too—one without the other is unacceptable. Too often, cooking is the neglected aspect, and that's just a crime. Smart layout and appliances must take top priority. A kitchen is really a cooking workshop, a utilitarian space for accomplishing a variety of tasks efficiently, with tools and appliances readily available.

The challenge, then, is to create an attractive room where one, two, or eight people can cook comfortably. For multi-cook kitchens, the layout should split the work load and permit good traffic flow. Two sinks, for separate preparation and cleanup, can double the size of a workspace without removing walls. In addition, the right appliances are essential, starting with heat. A cooktop should have suitable power at both the high *and* low ends of its heating spectrum. (Don't forget delicate sauces and simmering if you're a serious cook.) Those who bake or roast frequently will surely want a convection oven. The refrigerator and freezer, too, must be sufficient to house the foods the family most likes to prepare and eat.

Which comes first when you're designing a kitchen, selecting the cabinets or choosing the appliances?

Beautiful cabinets are nice, but again, the bottom line in the kitchen is cooking. Appliances determine the basic layout of a kitchen, so start there. For instance, where space is limited, a range is a great option; in larger kitchens, a separate cooktop and oven might be better. Myriad cabinet options make it easy to design around appliances, but homeowners who fall in love with cabinets and then try to find appliances to work with them are probably begging for trouble.

Many people know tons about the latest in kitchen equipment and appliances. They browse showrooms, take cooking classes, read informative books and attend product demonstrations; and this research gives these homeowners and their kitchen designers a leg up on the process. Everyone involved knows from the get-go that the kitchen will need, for example, a built-in steam oven, a coffee/cappuccino system, an indoor barbecue grill or a warming drawer, and as such, the design and planning process runs a lot more smoothly than if the installers have to squeeze in an appliance, as an afterthought.

What is the most overrated feature in kitchen design?

The kitchen triangle can be an obstacle to flexible, contemporary kitchen design. This static concept doesn't always adjust well to a space where several people will be working at once. When the concept was developed in the late 1940s, the idea was to make the most efficient use of small postwar kitchens by planning the room around a triangle formed by the three appliances of the day: refrigerator, sink, and stove. Today's kitchens have separate cooktops, wall ovens, microwaves, steamers, and much more, and these spaces don't always take kindly to triangles. Here is a more sensible design principle: A functional kitchen has the ability to take a given space and expand or compress the capacity of that space so it can respond to a given need at a given time. The "focal point" concept is overused, too. An element shouldn't stand out so much that people come in and say, "Wow, what a great countertop!" They should say, "Wow, what a great kitchen!"

Should the design of a kitchen coordinate or contrast with a home's decor?

Kitchen decor should definitely coordinate with the rest of a home whenever possible. Years ago, kitchens were often cubbies that were treated like service areas. Today's trend, both in new construction and remodeling projects, is to open kitchens onto surrounding living areas. Along with making the kitchen a social hub, this open look creates the need for kitchen design that flows into the overall style of your home.

How do you achieve this visual continuity?

Coordination of a kitchen and its surrounding areas comes through consciously striving for continuity of colors, materials, and textures, starting with the big things. This is where the homeowners' choice of cabinets plays a huge role. The cabinets should blend in style and color with the wood tones in the adjacent areas.

Another great idea is to bring furniture into the kitchen. For instance, an armoire can serve as a pantry. An old desk or pie chest can visually bridge two rooms *and* act as storage for bills, recipes, or maybe even pies.

If possible, bring fabrics from the the living areas into the kitchen, too, as cushions or window treatments. Delicate fabrics might appear in tiny accents or as trim. When blending colors, also blend textures, mixing and matching to add interest. Even materials like leather, which may seem a bit odd in a kitchen, can work—how about bordering a floor area with leather tiles? Repeat the stones and metals in living areas in kitchen drawer pulls, surfaces, and accents. A kitchen can be used to display a prized collection or to show off some interesting artwork, making it an extension of your tastes and interests. Often, these interests are already on display in the living room.

Before starting any installation, assemble a complete palette of materials—paint colors, wallpapers, fabrics swatches, carpet and flooring samples, and wood chips. Then, overlap the samples against a neutral surface to see how they work together. If one element sticks out, get rid of it and try something else. If there's a good flow, it's a pretty sure bet that collection of colors and fabrics is going to work together when installed.

How do trends influence kitchen design?

Homeowners are free to revel like sailors on leave in trendy design indulgences. They should remember, however, that a hangover awaits them when a) they get tired of those 24-karat gold-flecked cabinets; or b) it comes time to sell the home and the countertops are fire-engine red. In a kitchen, nearly everything is built-in, so following trends in color, style, or materials can be a costly mistake, especially come resell time. Most of today's popular materials—wood, stone, ceramic tile, laminate, cast iron, stainless steel, even solid surfacing—have stood the test of time and should remain popular.

Designers tend to discourage homeowners from getting too much of anything in a bright color, even if a client is totally in love with, say, red. The distance from "totally in love" to "color fatigued" is surprisingly short. Still, there is some wiggle room for the adventurous. For the hot red lover, one designer specified a red island, with a more sensible black granite for the main countertops and backsplashes. This was an effective compromise, and down the road, the island top will be much easier to replace than all the counters in the kitchen.

How does a designer meld the technical requirements of a kitchen with interior design?

The first step is to inventory the furniture, fabrics, colors, and art of the home to get a feel for the client's tastes. Just as important is the architecture. The owner of an English Tudor house who likes contemporary furnishings and is set on high-gloss lacquer cabinet doors would be well advised to compromise. Perhaps that person would accept frameless cabinets with a door style more befitting the period of the house. In designing a kitchen that will fit its setting, these issues have to be considered.

Exposed kitchen appliances can look fine in a contemporary home. But when the decor is traditional, consider concealing the appliances as much as possible. The most common option is to disguise them with panels to match the cabinets, but retro-style appliances are becoming more common. They have a period look, but their function is completely modern.

Try to make the built-ins—cabinets, island, hutch, sideboard, armoire—look like furniture by choosing woods, stains, paints, and counter materials that harmonize with the period of the house. Last, don't forget the backsplash. After all the cabinets and countertops have been specified, it's an empty canvas, a veritable playground of creativity. From European mosaic mural designs to contemporary artisan glass, a backsplash can be designed to suit any kitchen.

What is the biggest misconception that consumers have when they start redesigning their kitchen?

How much it will really cost! A basic 150- to 200-square-foot kitchen remodel might start at $30,000; done with luxury materials, it can jump to $80,000. Even those willing to do a little demolition work themselves and compromise on some products can easily spend in excess of $20,000. Retailers' ads in Sunday papers often quote cabinet prices only and are misleading. Final cost has to factor in all the other materials and, most important, labor. The total can come as a shock to those whose only knowledge of costs comes from looking at those ads. Remember, though, a car might cost $30,000, and a kitchen lasts longer.

Many clients are also confused about the designer's role. Kitchen design is a complex, detailed endeavor. It's not just about making the room look pretty; it's a delicate web of technical issues. Do most homeowners know the adequate wattage per square foot for lighting? Or whether to use standard or low-voltage fixtures? Or where to place electrical boxes? Clients who think they'll save money doing the entire job themselves can really come up short.

What trends do you see in kitchen cabinet design?

Bold, old-world designs, while beautiful, are giving way to a relaxed style. Mission, Arts and Crafts, and Shaker cabinets reflect this trend while still creating warmth and charm.

Three- and four-layer crown molding is giving way to cove and straight-line molding. Carved corbels and ornate range hoods, once standard, are being replaced by straight-line styles. Details that enhance a sense of craftsmanship are in demand, including inlays, chamfered or beveled edges (square edges trimmed at a 45-degree angle), and pegged doors (with hickory pegs inserted in the corners).

Of course, trends are always cyclical. Ornate details could come back at any time, although Shaker does seem to have a certain staying power.

What's your advice on appliances and hardware?

Stainless steel is excellent—in moderation! A refrigerator and dishwasher hidden behind cabinet panels would get a lovely complement from stainless steel ovens, microwaves, and warming drawers. For a larger dose, refrigerators now come in stainless steel finishes that hide fingerprints. These appliances will survive the test of time to become classics.

The return of brightly colored appliances, however, may turn out to be short-lived. Red, blue, or orange refrigerators or ranges may wear out their welcome long before the cabinets or countertops. (Remember avocado and harvest gold?) Prudence says accessories and small appliances are the best ways to add bright color to a kitchen.

Hardware selection can be as time-consuming as settling on cabinet style and finish. The most important consideration for hardware is that it complements the entire room. The non-polished, silver-color finishes, for instance—pewter, stainless steel, brushed chrome, or the more subtle satin nickel—are appropriate in nearly any setting. Look for PVD (physical vapor deposition) finishes in hardware and other metal accessories, especially if you're shopping for polished brass. The finish locks in the tone and sheen of the surface, eliminating scratches and oxidation.

How should a person use innovative products in a kitchen remodel?

As professional-style cooking equipment rose in popularity, the questions started coming: "Do we really need fancy gear if we eat out all the time?" Homeowners absolutely *must* take stock of what equipment will work for their situation. People who like to draw the family into their homes for big meals that involve lots of pots and baked goods…go ahead and get that restaurant-style range. On the other hand, families that don't sit down to eat together—which, alas, seems to be the norm these days—can skip the monster oven and go for a built-in warming drawer so late-comers can have food that's still hot but not recooked or dried out. Ovens with temperature probes and programmable cooking modes are error-proof and can really help a person become a better cook. One American plumbing giant makes a sink that cooks; the basin holds an 8-quart pot that's filled, heated, and drained in place, with no need to haul it between the stove and the main sink. It's great for two-cook kitchens.

Many environmentally friendly innovations are in laundry appliances. The trend toward more efficient, water-saving washing machines and dryers started in Europe and has made its way to the U.S. These machines are electronically savvy; when properly used do a better job of washing, and treat clothes more gently than traditional models.

What innovations for the kitchen will have the most impact in the next decade?

Computers and automation are going to have profound effects. Companies keep computerized inventories—why shouldn't households? The infrastructure isn't there yet, but as it is built, computers would be able to keep track of what's in refrigerators and pantries and call the supermarket when supplies run low. Every item the family consumes, the scenario goes, would be scanned and added to the replenishing list. At the appropriate time, the home shopper would activate the order to buy and either go pick up the groceries or have them delivered.

Maybe all this won't be in place within the next decade, but it seems perfectly feasible. Already, computer monitors are dropping from below cabinets and being built into refrigerator fronts. These audio-visual systems can handle TV, radio, DVD, CD, Internet, e-mail, home-security and even baby-monitoring duties.

Kitchens
for
Cooking

All dressed up for a function

THE GOLD STANDARD FOR ANY KITCHEN is functionality, and that means gobs of storage, appliances, and plenty of space for meal prep. This kitchen needed all of this without adding square footage. Robin Siegerman, CKD, of Sieguzi Interior Designs in Toronto, tackled this challenge while returning a "remuddled" kitchen to some semblance of the home's original Arts and Crafts style.

Garish 1970s-era chic—a scarlet sink and white cabinets—clashed painfully with the rest of the home. Even worse, functional deficiencies thwarted the utility of the room: A large microwave and small appliances ate up counter space, and a table created bottlenecks in the aisle between the base cabinets and a bump-out. The homeowners got rid of the table by requesting a family room and breakfast nook off the kitchen, but this move also risked an awkward transition between the kitchen and the new room through the oddly shaped bump-out.

The homeowners also wanted an island and a return to the Arts and Crafts roots of the home. Because she couldn't really re-create such a style, Siegerman instead reinterpreted. Recognizing the kitchen as too narrow for an island, she filled it with easy-to-access storage and generous countertops. To smooth the transition from kitchen to family room, she transformed the bump-out into a closet and telephone nook.

Rather than reproducing an early-20th-century style note for note, Siegerman evoked it instead, with recessed door panels, custom molding, a stained-wood finish for the range hood, and a divided-light window that visually ties the kitchen with the wood-paneled butler's pantry. To keep the north-facing room from becoming too dark, she mixed plenty of light-reflecting surfaces and compatible wood cabinets.

The other half of the job—bringing the kitchen up to date—

required fitting new appliances and modern materials into the design. To this end, a new 48-inch side-by-side refrigerator was paired with a microwave oven (conveniently tucked into an upper cabinet to conserve countertop space), and a stainless steel double wall-oven was placed next to a new baking center. Amber-colored granite counters extend in a spacious U shape from the fridge all the way around the room to the pullout pantry on the opposite wall, providing acres of contiguous work surface.

The thoughtful mix of storage areas keeps small appliances off the countertops and provides undercabinet space for everything from seasonings to recycling bins. A full-height pullout pantry by the double oven supplies ample shelf space for food, while swing-out corner cabinet units and deep drawers under the cooktop create convenient access to oversize pots and pans. Narrow pullouts on either side of these deep drawers keep spices and condiments within easy reach; rollout trash and recycling receptacles simplify package and container disposal.

Siegerman says the finished space is casual, yet sophisticated and efficient enough for two or three people to work in at the same time without getting in one another's way. Throw in room for a couple of cooks and young helpers, too, and that's a combination of comfort and functionality everyone can appreciate.

PRECEDING PAGES:
Vertical bands of ivory cabinets lighten the kitchen. Stained-wood trim, cabinet faces, and window mullions tie the renovated kitchen to its home's Arts and Crafts heritage.

ABOVE: A stainless steel dishwasher and sink reflect light in the north-facing kitchen enhancing the appeal of the divided-light windows.

WHAT DESIGNS DOES STAINLESS STEEL COMPLEMENT?
Stainless steel is certainly a high-tech material, a much more modern product than concrete (which, after all, was invented by the ancient Romans). Softer metals, such as copper and zinc, convey a classic feeling, a sense of history—think of the verdigris copper roof of a cathedral, or the zinc bar in an old Paris bistro—but stainless steel more or less shouts contemporary.

RIGHT: With the addition of a cabinet and some open shelving, a small, potentially awkward triangular space becomes a useful nook for the telephone and cookbooks.

ABOVE: Swing-out units of sturdy steel-wire shelving allow easy access to even the darkest corners of the base cabinets.

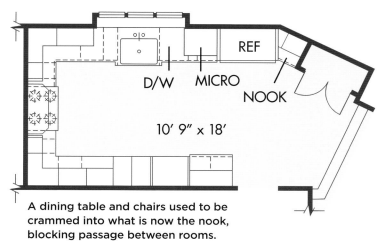

A dining table and chairs used to be crammed into what is now the nook, blocking passage between rooms.

From Brady to French Country

SHORTLY AFTER BETH AND JUDSON BERTOCH purchased a 30-year-old house in Reston, Virginia, they realized the kitchen had to go. "It was your typical *Brady Bunch* room with lots of laminate and zero storage," says Judson, evoking an era when kitchens didn't have runway-length countertops and pull-out pantries.

The first-time remodelers turned to designer Jennifer Day, CKD, for answers. After addressing specific needs and discussing user-friendly alternatives, the couple decided to gut the cramped 10x12-foot space and start over. Topping the wish list: room for storage and a spot for casual dining.

The linchpin of the 140-square-foot space is a custom-designed island. The granite-topped unit is multifunctional—pinch-hitting as additional work space, informal eating area, or convenient off-loading spot for groceries. "We deliberately kept it simple," says Beth of the two-tiered design. The lower level is used for casual dining; at the opposite end, the counter is raised 6 inches, allowing strategic placement of power outlets, which come in handy when using electrical appliances.

The clients gravitated toward a breezy French Country style, selecting creamy yellow cabinets with simple recessed-panel doors. "When Judson spotted the yellow cabinets, we didn't look any further," says Beth, noting that as principal cook, Judson had the final say in most of the design decisions.

The couple experimented with several colors before deciding on a deep cinnabar shade for the walls. "Initially, it took some getting used to," says Beth. "Now we love the warmth and depth the color gives the space. After all these months of eating out, we've finally got a great place to come home to." And that's the way this space became the un-Brady kitchen.

PRECEDING PAGES: Honey-colored teak floors, richly textured granite counters, sills, and backsplashes, and stainless steel appliances complement the classic lines of the Provençal-inspired cabinetry

ABOVE: The 5x3-foot granite-topped island has furniture-style details, including beadboard side panels and bracket-mounted legs. The hard-working unit does triple duty, providing space for dining, prep chores, and storage.

ISLAND INSIGHTS

DOUBLING UP Two tiers maximize the work surface on the island, allowing one portion of the counter to serve as a prep station and the other as an eating area.
POWER PLAY Small appliances hide behind paneled doors where they can be accessed easily. Built-in electrical outlets provide additional "plug-in" power.
BAKER'S BOON The cool, smooth granite countertop on the island makes it an ideal surface for working with chilled doughs for piecrusts, puff pastries, and cookies.

RIGHT: A narrow cabinet stores spices. Why so tall? To pick up the strong vertical of the vent hood is one reason, but mainly it's because the wall cabinets on the other side of the hood are that height, too.

ABOVE, TOP TO BOTTOM: A drop-down cookbook holder frees up counter space. Dishwasher drawers save room and energy compared with their full-size counterparts. Ideally, every kitchen would have a warming drawer. Among its uses: It keeps dinner warm for latecomers.

GREAT STORAGE IDEAS

CHEF'S DRAWER A drawer deep enough to hold bottles of oil, vinegar, and whatever spices and utensils the cook uses most frequently. Locating it next to the range keeps its contents handy.

DIAGONAL PULLOUTS Rather than circular lazy Susans, which waste corner space, install rectangular shelves that pull out diagonally. Mounting them on heavy-duty, full-extension glides lets you stow even the weightiest pots and pans.

CONCEALED SPICE DRAWER Storage can be both decorative and functional. Small columns flanking the range carry through the classic column motif. The pullout filler pantry nearest the range also holds seasonings and condiments.

UNOBTRUSIVE WINE STORAGE Installing the wine cooler behind a cabinet doorframe with a furniture-look footed toekick allows it to blend in with the cabinetry. Wines that do not need to be cooled can be stored in a cupboard.

TOWEL NICHE To avoid the unsightly look of a damp towel untidily draped over an oven door handle, install a hook or rod in a niche in the cabinetry.

Delights of the round table

REDESIGNING A KITCHEN to accommodate a favorite piece of furniture may be putting the proverbial cart in front of the horse, but that's exactly what homeowners Sarah and Jeff Millar of Shrewsbury, Massachusetts, did when they spied a vintage marble-topped table at an auction. "I liked its proportions," says Sarah, who admits that the purchase sat in a corner of the living room for two years before it found a permanent home. "We ended up having to build a whole new room around it," she says.

With five children under age 14, family activities figured prominently on the Millars' priority list. Their expansive Mediterranean-style home, built in the early 1920s, was perfect for raising a family, but the kitchen lacked modern amenities and space for casual dining. Eating together was important to the family, according to designer Fran Garofoli, CKD, who helped mastermind the new design. They needed a functional, efficient space, one that was compatible with the period of the home but could accommodate the demands of a family as well.

Working with architect Daniel Benoit, the couple approved plans for a 140-square-foot addition that doubled the size of the kitchen and linked it to the adjacent family room. "I didn't want anything that screamed new construction," says Sarah, who insisted on retaining as much of the original flavor as possible. "This wasn't meant to be an elaborate room; it was strictly utilitarian—a service kitchen." To impart a feeling of age, columns separate the working part of the kitchen from the dining area and are repeated again at the juncture leading to the family room, providing both vertical interest and visual heft.

Keeping with the warm woods and simple lines of the original butler's pantry, Sarah selected traditional recessed-panel maple cabinets in an antique white enamel and dark mahogany stain.

PRECEDING PAGES:
The floor plan flows easily
between the kitchen
and the dining table.
Architectural details
such as the coffered
ceiling, sets of columns,
and contrasting ceiling
molding evoke authentic
1920s-era charm.

RIGHT: Blending light and
dark cabinetry finishes
plays off the color scheme
suggested by the white
ceiling and the plank floor.

TABLE TALK

Although appliance and cabinet
selection demands a big chunk
of both money and time, thinking
about where the family will eat
together is just as important.
If meals are eaten at an island or
peninsula, it will need some type
of pull-up seating; if the plan calls
for gathering at a table, consider
its size, shape, and style.

Although square or rectangular
tables are common, homeowners
Jeff and Sarah Millar were drawn
to the intimacy their round table
provides (see pp. 28–29). "When
you put six or eight people at a
rectangular table, it tends to limit
group conversation," Sarah says.
For comfortable seating, allow
a width of 24 to 30 inches per
person. Parents of small children
should also consider the safety
benefit: Round tables have no
sharp corners. For their brood,
Jeff and Sarah opted for a 6-foot-
diameter marble top anchored
to a sturdy base. The table also
doubles as a convenient spot for
homework or board games.

A mix of open and closed cupboards, a custom-built pantry closet, and an old-fashioned plate rack—within easy reach of the extra-deep soapstone sink—provide storage and maintain period authenticity and charm.

The anchor of the U-shaped floor plan is a three-tiered island with a dishwasher, prep sink, and storage. It serves as the kitchen's central work zone. To deter trespassing into the cook's space, the children's snacks and beverages are kept in a refrigerator concealed in the built-in pantry on the opposite wall. This allows the children to help themselves to their favorite snacks and drinks without getting in the way.

Family meals take place at the expansive marble-topped pedestal table that sparked the whole remodeling project. Directly above the table, a 6x6-foot skylight, resembling a traditional cupola, provides plenty of natural light. Sunshine fills every corner of the room, making it cheery, even on cloudy New England days. "I think the kitchen's warmth is enhanced by the bustle of our large family," says Sarah. "I could never have imagined how much more alive our home could be."

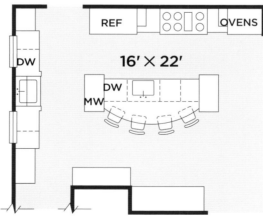

With the microwave at the end of the island, kids don't have to cut through the kitchen to heat up snacks.

With three principal work aisles—including an ample push-back area for seating at the breakfast bar—the kitchen can easily accommodate multiple cooks.

46 WAYS TO STREAMLINE YOUR KITCHEN

SAY GOODBYE TO THAT CROWDED, CLUTTERED KITCHEN. These handy suggestions for streamlining the space will increase efficiency, effectively integrate decorative touches, and update the decor.

REDUCE CLUTTER

Use an over-the-door pantry organizer to free up room on counter-tops and in cabinets.

- Build an appliance garage with a tambour door to hide such appliances as a toaster, can or jar opener, coffeemaker, or blender.
- Hang hooks for dish towels or small utensils inside cabinet doors.
- Install a tilt-out storage tray (a standard installation kit is available at home centers) behind the false-front panel in front of the sink.
- Store a step stool in the toekick space under cabinets.
- Build a banquette along one wall for seating and as an underseat storage area for oversize and infrequently used pots, bowls, and trays.
- Hang a plate rack over the sink.
- Coordinate containers so they can "fade" into the background, even if they're attractive.

- Purchase sleek, touch-lid trash cans for easy disposal if you haven't got room for a compactor.
- Replace a butcher-block knife holder with a wall-mounted, magnetic strip; hang it well out of the reach of small children.
- Fit drawers with spice racks to hide a plethora of different containers.
- Keep counters clear, and file family mail and keys in wall cubbies.
- Dry towels on a wall-mounted dish-towel rack that folds flat when you're not using it.
- Mount a paper-towel holder under a cabinet or on the inside of a door.
- Save space with an over-the-sink chopping board and built-in colander.
- Incorporate undercounter trays to hold glassware so it can be handy but out of sight.

An undercounter rack helps organize your most-used spices.

MAKE DECORATIVE TOUCHES COUNT

• Accessorize with a few distinctive, eye-catching pieces rather than cluttering the space with lots of smaller items.

• Maximize the impact of a collection without overwhelming the space by displaying items on one wall or on specially designed shelves.

• Choose matching frames for posters or artwork.

• Build shallow wall niches to show off collectibles.

• Cover chair seats with tailored (rather than ruffled) cushions.

• Corral frequently used utensils in a single large urn or pitcher.

• Transfer dishwashing detergent to an attractive bottle with spout.

• Cover a table with a single runner rather than layering it with several cumbersome cloths.

• Store extra linens, napkins, and cutlery in wicker baskets neatly lined up along open shelves.

• Replace lots of little scatter rugs with a single large one.

• Give postcards, recipes, and photographs a home on a sleek stainless steel magnetic board.

• Build shelves on the side of an island or peninsula to hold favorite cookbooks and often-used utensils.

• Paint or stain stools or chairs the same color as the walls, appliances, or floors so they blend in.

LET IN THE LIGHT

• Hang simple Roman shades to cover the windows.

• Consider shades or blinds that disappear under a coordinated headrail when raised.

• Hang glass shelves across windows to display interesting bottles, containers, and vases.

• Use mini-pendant lights over islands or peninsulas for effective, not overpowering illumination.

• Install pulley lights that you can raise or lower as desired.

OPEN UP THE SPACE

• Keep flooring simple and natural; avoid busy patterns.

• Use a monochromatic color scheme for the walls.

• Install stainless steel appliances for a sleek, contemporary look (not necessarily a restaurant look).

• Strike a modern note with crisp colors and metallic accents and accessories.

• Replace obtrusive or gaudy cabinet hardware with simple white porcelain knobs or matte-finish pulls in stainless steel or nickel.

• Use smooth-fronted cabinet doors for an aesthetically pleasing sense of coordination.

• Choose muted, matte materials for countertop surfaces.

• Choose an undermount sink to give your countertop a smooth, continuous look.

• Run cabinets up to the ceiling.

• Order custom panels for appliances to allow them to blend in with the cabinets.

• Choose a smooth-top range for its unobtrusive surface.

• Add simple shelving around the perimeter of the room for bowls, pitchers and other vessels.

• Open the upper half of the room by avoiding wall cabinets altogether. Store items that would go in those cabinets on open shelves or in a pantry in a nearby room.

Self-stick hooks and clips give your kitchen more versatility.

Small wonder

WITH THE APPROXIMATE COMFORT LEVEL of a phone booth and everything rapidly deteriorating, the problems in the kitchen of Bonnie Gerow and Colin Berryman's 1978 town house in Toronto were not difficult to comprehend. "We both like to cook, but we couldn't fit in there at the same time," says Bonnie. "If one person was cooking, the other couldn't even come in to get a drink or some ice cubes." Less frustrating—but still far from pleasing—was how the room looked. The finish on the pressed-board cabinets was peeling, and the once-dramatic black floor tiles had dulled to a grimy gray. Finally, insufficient storage left the room cluttered and claustrophobic.

Enter designer Erica Westeroth, CKD. Unable to enlarge the footprint of the kitchen—the little town house left no room for expansion—Westeroth did the next best thing: She arranged major appliances and work centers around the perimeter of the room in a pattern that prevents Bonnie and Colin from tripping over each other. In addition, by removing a small dividing wall, replacing a standard-size refrigerator with a counter-height model, and partly recessing the microwave into the wall, Westeroth cleared out a few more precious inches of space.

As important to Bonnie and Colin as the layout were the finishing touches in the room. Simple maple cabinets with clean lines complement the modern style of the house, and a few accents of color add just the right pizzazz. Picking up on the blue flecks in the black granite countertops—"We saw that beautiful countertop and latched on to it right away," says Bonnie—Westeroth designed a medley of blue tiles for the backsplash over the range. Stonelike porcelain tiles on the floor also display subtle bits of blue. The end product is a sure success. "Now that we can really use our kitchen, we're having a lot of home-cooked meals," says Bonnie.

OPPOSITE: In a tiny kitchen, cabinets with simple lines and a light, friendly maple finish don't overwhelm.

BELOW: A built-in chopping block sits at a step-saving location in the kitchen— the midpoint of the counter that separates the range and the sink.

OPPOSITE: A greenhouse-style window floods the working areas of the room with that most valuable and elusive asset in a kitchen: natural light.

RIGHT: Paring down the materials palette—this kitchen has one wood, one metal, and three color-coordinated surfaces—keeps the small space uncomplicated.-

BELOW: Strategically located between the microwave and the range, a small counter area is a perfect place to set down dishes hot from the oven.

MAKE THE MOST OF A COMPACT SPACE

RESIST THE TEMPTATION to maximize storage space by lining the walls with rows of cabinets. The room will look too closed in, the designer says. Instead, go for a balance between what she calls negative and positive space. By including some open wall space—like shelves, for instance—the kitchen will feel more spacious.

STORE COOKING SUPPLIES close to where they'll be used. An undercounter cabinet next to the range in this kitchen, for example, pulls out to reveal a stash of cooking oils and sprays.

CHOOSE FIXTURES with clean lines that won't create visual clutter. The cabinets here are completely unadorned, while the range features a sleek design.

OPPOSITE: One virtue of a small kitchen is that everything is within reach for a single cook; the problems arise when more than one person works in the room. Foot traffic can be controlled when there are distinct task areas spread throughout the space.

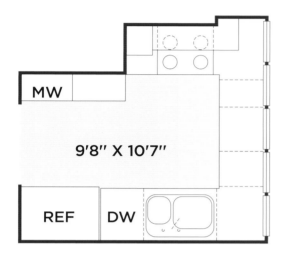

9'8" X 10'7"

MW

REF   DW

ABOVE: Although it wasn't possible to physically expand the kitchen, rearranging the floor plan did wonders for the room's efficiency. Workstations are now laid out in a logical sequence around the edges of the kitchen. Food prep goes in a tidy counterclockwise motion, from refrigerator to sink (if needed) to butcher-block cutting board to range. Then (again, if needed) the cook can turn around and return to the sink to clean up.

RIGHT: A random pattern of simple ceramic tiles in a range of blues adds color to the kitchen. The backsplash takes its hue cue from the chips found throughout the granite countertop.

VISUALLY EXPAND THE KITCHEN IN SMALL SPACES

BRING THE WINDOWS DOWN to counter height—typically 39 inches above the floor.

IF THE SINK IS AT A WINDOW, box out the window to give a feeling of space behind the counter, and consider fitting the extended area with recessed window boxes for seasonal plants. To make things simpler, decide on a single countertop surface and cabinet finish, and choose just one focal point— such as artwork or an important appliance.

KEEP THE EYE MOVING within the kitchen, paint the ceiling in a lighter shade of the wall color, and use cabinet panels to disguise appliances. Creating sight lines into another space, whether it be the outdoors or the next room, is important.

ALONG THE SAME LINES, hide plug moldings under wall cabinets, eliminating electrical outlets in the backsplash that stop the eye and interrupt the design. It's possible for a small kitchen to express a big personality if it makes a real statement with color or theme.

Mighty mite

WHEN THESE TORONTO HOMEOWNERS first asked designer Erica Westeroth, CKD, for help reworking their 100-square-foot kitchen, they knew the project posed a unique set of problems. First off, from a designer's point of view, the kitchen was smaller than a small kitchen—it was a mini-kitchen. A small kitchen is certainly a design challenge, but a mini is an invitation to a migraine. On top of that, the kitchen was populated with dense, tobacco-brown cabinets and 30-year-old appliances.

As if the petite proportions and baleful built-ins weren't daunting enough, the homeowners had an extensive wish list that had to be incorporated into the remodel. The couple wanted not only to update the 1970s appearance of the room; they wanted to block views of an unsightly staircase that ran to the basement; to increase counter space; to add an eating area; to incorporate hidden storage for small appliances; and to provide concealed accommodations for appliances, including a side-by-side stainless steel refrigerator. In sum, they weren't willing to forgo any full-size kitchen features, regardless of their kitchen's size.

Westeroth faced one restriction on the project: She couldn't expand the kitchen—not because the couple wouldn't allow it, but simply because there was no place to go. If she had expanded into the front hall, the front door would have been blocked. To the right was a staircase that couldn't be moved, and to the left was the dining room.

Westeroth was able to knock an opening in the wall that separates the galley-style kitchen from the formal dining room. The original purpose of this opening was to visually

OPPOSITE: The range that commands one wall of the room has a front control panel rather than a raised backsplash design. Using a low-profile appliance like this one preserves the clean lines along the perimeter of the room.

BELOW: Cozy seating for two is provided at the border of the kitchen.

ABOVE: A series of small framed openings in the wall behind the sink combat the claustrophobic feel of the kitchen. These "windows" continue the geometric theme of the room and prevent a boxed-in feeling.

RIGHT: Walls are put to work with a simple hanging-rod storage system for cooking utensils.

BELOW, RIGHT: Available in 3-inch increments, pullout-pantry cabinet fillers make even awkward bits of leftover space productive.

FAR RIGHT: A simple countertop cabinet hides frequently used items from view but keeps them at hand.

WHAT MAKES IT WORK?

DOWNPLAY DECORATIVE DETAILS Keep trim to a minimum to cut down on visual clutter, which can make a room feel smaller because it doesn't allow your eyes to rest, according to designer Erica Westeroth. In this kitchen, she specified flat-front cabinets for a simple, sophisticated facade that recedes into the background.

A NEW SLANT Instead of setting the square floor tiles on a strict horizontal grid, Westeroth chose to place them on the diagonal. Such a pattern fools the eye into thinking the walls have been pushed out, even though they really haven't, she says.

BREAK DOWN BARRIERS To fill the dark space with much-needed natural light and connect it with the rest of the house, Westeroth carved out an opening in the wall that separates the kitchen from the dining room.

STOCK UP ON STORAGE Clear counters allow a kitchen to breathe. To that end, in this kitchen Westeroth included plenty of drawers for concealing everything from cutlery to pots and pans. She also installed metal rods along the backsplash for hanging pot holders and utensils.

enlarge the narrow room by providing views of the backyard. Once the opening was in place, however, Westeroth discovered the counter area it left behind could be used as a breakfast bar with enough room to comfortably seat two.

A new wall behind the sink thankfully obscured the view of the basement staircase. The designer also increased the depth of the sink-side countertop by several inches to make room for a garage-style cupboard for hiding idle small appliances. The added depth also allowed room to install the microwave oven flush with the surrounding cabinets.

Appliance placement follows the standard layout of a U-shaped floor plan, with the range centered at the top and the refrigerator, sink, and dishwasher to the sides. To minimize the intrusion of the oversize refrigerator, Westeroth recessed the appliance into an alcove. The resulting effect is a successful imitation of a built-in installation.

To finish the kitchen, the designer selected sophisticated but playful colors like brilliant blues, soft greens, and sleek silvers. Cherry cabinets with a simple flat front add to the contemporary twist.

RIGHT: Once the wall between the kitchen and the dining room came down, it was possible to widen the counter on that side of the room, creating an intimate space for dining.

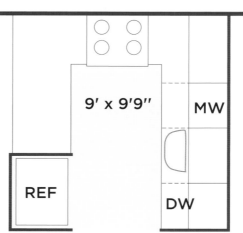

9' x 9'9"

MW

REF

DW

ABOVE: Smooth-front cabinets, with a distinct vertical grain and minimalist hardware, encourage the eye to continuously scan the 100-square-foot room.

55 WAYS TO MAKE YOUR KITCHEN A COOK'S HAVEN

A RESTAURANT KITCHEN ISN'T NECESSARY to feed family and friends, but an attractive, organized, well-equipped space ensures that the kitchen is a haven for all who gather there—especially the chef! Here are some ideas to make your kitchen cook-friendly.

A plate rack provides pretty storage and easy access to bakeware and dishes.

- Analyze the space for efficient work flow. Sometimes simply moving an appliance cuts down on unnecessary steps.
- Outfit a section of countertop with a marble slab for baking.
- Replace wooden panels in kitchen cabinet doors with glass inserts to show off favorite dishes.
- Install fitted compartments in kitchen drawers for spices, cutlery, and cleaning supplies.
- Splurge on granite countertops, at least for the areas on either side of the stove, to hold hot pots, bowls, and casserole dishes.
- Replace a standard kitchen faucet with a high gooseneck version to make filling deep pots easier.
- Install a second sink for cleanup.
- Slide a wine refrigerator under one section of a counter or island.
- Attach a special magnetic strip to a wall to hold kitchen knives.
- Turn a small corner into an office complete with a computer for the organized cook. Add cookbooks and reference items to the space.
- Find room for a rocker or other comfortable chair for a weary cook.
- Update cabinets with sliding shelves for easy access to supplies.
- Hang a pot rack over an island.
- Install storage grids along one wall to hold pot lids and miscellaneous kitchen equipment.
- Replace shallow drawers with deep ones for pot storage.
- Keep frequently used equipment such as coffeemakers, mixers, and food processors handy yet out of sight with appliance garages.
- Add shelves for cookbooks.
- Store grains, rice, and beans in drawers with glass fronts for both textural appeal and practicality. You'll always know when to restock.
- Arrange frequently used dishes and equipment attractively on open stainless steel shelving.
- Add a wall oven.
- Accommodate extra-large cookware with an extra-deep sink.
- Install glass shelves high in a kitchen window to allow glassware to catch the light.
- Have shallow shelves built to hold platters and trays.
- Customize drawers with functional wooden inserts.
- Transform the toekick space near an oven into a drawer for cookie tins and baking dishes.
- Attach locking casters onto heavy worktables for easier mobility.
- Choose adjustable shelves.
- Build cabinets up to the ceiling. Access the items stored inside via a rolling library ladder.
- Find space for a small television so cooks can keep up with the news or their favorite shows.
- Opt for full-extension slides on all drawers so items don't slip to the back and get lost.
- Keep spatulas and wooden spoons in storage crocks or jars near the stove.
- Mount a pull-down cookbook holder under a cabinet, or tuck books underneath an island.

- Have sinks outfitted with a vegetable sprayer, either as part of the faucet or as an individual unit.
- Install a water source near the stove for filling oversize pots.
- Vary countertop surfaces to meet your needs: Ceramic tiles add texture to an island; stainless steel is great for food-prep areas—you can thoroughly scrub it; granite is excellent for receiving hot pots near the stove; and butcher block is the classic material for a cutting-board area.
- House back issues of cooking magazines and useful catalogs in attractive boxes, baskets, or bins.
- Pipe in music, or install a combination radio/CD player.
- Provide stools or seats for visitors.
- Illuminate the counters with undercabinet lights.
- Decorate the kitchen to reflect the personality and culinary interests of the chef.
- Consider the height of the cook when planning the height of the counters: Taller cooks need higher work surfaces.
- Outfit the sink with a customized cutting board so vegetable peelings and waste can be swept right down the drain immediately.
- Fit the overlooked space above the refrigerator with vertical dividers to hold trays.
- Store vegetables in wicker baskets with handles on open shelves.
- Install a plate rack over the sink for easy draining and storage.
- Hang a chalkboard on the wall to announce the day's menu.
- Place a microwave oven under the counter so kids can access it easily.
- Retrofit the space under the sink with sliders to hold trash containers and recycling bins.
- Install dimmers to provide the ideal dining ambience after the work is done.
- Protect walls from spots and stains with durable enamel paint that stands up to frequent washing.
- Add a trough sink to an island.

- Spotlight cabinets with track or recessed lighting.
- Attach a hinged half-circle surface to a cabinet end. Snap up for snacking or light meals.
- Organize work areas, such as a baking area, prep station, or beverage corner, for maximum efficiency. Store all the equipment you'll need nearby for easy access.
- Add an undercounter refrigerator to hold extra beverages, meats, cheeses, or produce for parties.

A pullout pantry organizes kitchen essentials.

Kitchens
for
Families

Small, dark and handsome

EXTRA-WIDE REFRIGERATORS and commercial-style cooktops are the stuff of big kitchens. Those stuck with small kitchens just have to make do. That's conventional wisdom.

This kitchen says, "Sorry, conventional wisdom." Thanks to a reworked floor plan and a clever cabinet treatment, Meredith and Dan Frankum of Franklin, Tennessee, got all the big appliances they wanted plus a sensible traffic pattern and a style that, at long last, matches their Tudor home.

Designer Melissa Smith, CKD, likens the home's exterior of stone, dark wood, and beveled glass to a European cottage. The light woods and generic finishes of the old kitchen just didn't make sense with that exterior. Cabinet doors were almond colored with wooden handles. White walls were stenciled in peach and mint green. A peninsula jutted into the main traffic lane. The homeowners wanted a better seating area for their three kids. It was a kitchen hopelessly, helplessly trapped in another time. The designer said it was awful, that there was nothing about it that was Tudor or evocative of a cottage. Simply put, the old kitchen just didn't do the house justice.

Meredith knew premium appliances clashed with her kitchen's size. "I didn't want it to look like wall-to-wall appliances," she says. Still, she wanted the best of both function and appearance. She had owned a Sub-Zero refrigerator before and was in love with its capacity and the fact that it could take cabinet panels to blend in with the room. In fact, Smith's choice of dishwasher appealed to the Frankums precisely because it could be paneled.

The space and appliance requirements did limit Smith's design options in terms of the floor plan. "There are only so many places a 42-inch refrigerator will fit," she notes. Once she mapped out the appliances and put the peninsula on the opposite wall, the layout was pretty much set.

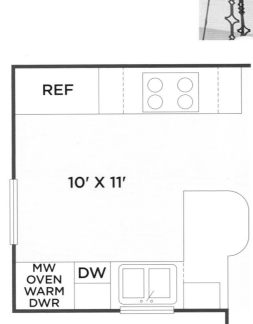

REF

10' X 11'

MW
OVEN
WARM
DWR

DW

Moving the peninsula to the other side of the room not only freed up the flow of foot traffic, but also formed the basis for a new and improved configuration for the seating arrangements in the remodeled kitchen.

PRECEDING PAGES: Fitting a 42-inch, built-in refrigerator and a big commercial-style cooktop in such a limited space is a major feat. This kitchen pulls it off, and throws in a double oven and warming drawer, for good measure.

RIGHT: Replete in rich wood and hewed stone, the kitchen is now in stylistic step with the house's historic architectural character.

Storage remained a challenge, though. So Smith commandeered an adjacent utility room for use as a pantry and flanked the cooktop with counter cabinets. Cannily, she didn't bring the stonework all the way down from over the cooktop, which allowed her to add storage in the form of two cabinets with pullout racks.

The primary purpose of the stone above the cooktop, in fact, is visual: Smith convinced the Frankums that their kitchen needed to complement the style of their Tudor home. The stone and dark cabinets set the tone of the decor. Smith avoided the somber, oppressive mood that dark cabinets can produce by bringing in more natural light and plenty of recessed ceiling fixtures, while lightening up the other surfaces, like the wall, floor, and countertops.

Speaking of countertops, the extra-deep counter that hangs out over the peninsula is an outstanding landing area for groceries. For seating, Smith put a wraparound bench into the existing breakfast nook—a big hit with the Frankums. "Scooting chairs in and out is a hassle," Meredith says. "Also, you can fit more people, especially kids, on the bench."

Add some beveled glass in the windows, and the kitchen truly fits its Tudor surroundings. And best of all, it has large appliances and an abundance of storage—just as a small kitchen should.

ABOVE: When selecting a dishwasher that will be fitted for a cabinet panel, look for appliances that have the controls on the top edge of the door. The finished look will be more polished than if the buttons and dials are on the front of the door.

RIGHT: No need to sacrifice specialized storage in a small kitchen. Tucked under one of the beveled-glass-front cabinets (a nod to the Tudoresque details in other parts of the house), an appliance garage sports a flip-up door. A side-hinged design would eat into the counter area.

SMALL KITCHEN SMARTS

EXTEND CABINETS UP TO THE CEILING Not only will this provide long-term storage for little-used items, it also makes the room appear larger.
CONCEAL THE APPLIANCES Using coordinating cabinetry panels on the fronts of the fridge and dishwasher will give the space a more coherent look.
MAKE THE BEST USE OF A PENINSULA Using a wider countertop, as designer Melissa Smith did, provides more landing space for groceries. With doors on both sides of the peninsula, people can access the cabinets' contents without getting in the way of the busy cook.

Adding a wall of stone connects the kitchen in a material sense to the exterior of the home. To allow for additional storage, the stonework doesn't extend down to the counter.

French open

EVEN CLOSE FAMILIES NEED SPACE. Eileen and Charlie Connolly and their two children, Kevin and Maggie, enjoy each other's company so much that they like to be together even during meal preparation. Cooking together, however, was more chaos than pleasant, communal activity before the Connollys undertook a six-month-long gut renovation of the kitchen in their house in Glen Ellyn, Illinois.

"We always seemed to be running into each other," says Eileen. "I wanted my kids to be in the kitchen with me doing their homework, but just not in the way while I was making dinner." Even though the kitchen expanded modestly—from 210 to 272 square feet—"the change made a huge difference," says Eileen.

The project was less about creating more area than it was improving the traffic flow. When the Connollys moved into the 3,500-square-foot, 1939 French Normandy–style house years ago, they resigned themselves to living with the kitchen, despite its drab appearance. It was a room rife with dark oak and walnut, faded linoleum, and scuffed laminate counters; and it was defined by an unwieldy U-shaped peninsula that Eileen recalls as being "a constant cause of congestion."

When the Connollys hired David McFadden and Jennifer McKnight, kitchen designers at Past Basket in Geneva, Illinois, Eileen knew she wanted an island instead of a peninsula. In fashioning the island, McFadden and McKnight found the narrowness of the kitchen to be a real challenge. The team designed a 2-foot-wide, teak-topped unit, as opposed to one with a standard 3-foot width. Keeping to a strict policy to preserve open space in the room, the designers opted for floor-to-ceiling cabinetry that was shallower than usual. Typical tall cabinets are 24 inches deep, but the ones in this kitchen vary from 12 to 14 inches deep, meaning they protrude less.

Every aspect of the cabinets received careful consideration, from shelf position to the way every door opens. A unit adjacent to the

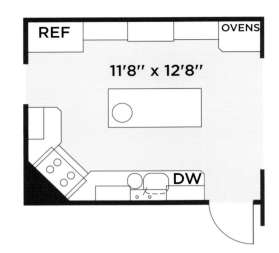

PRECEDING PAGES: Removing a peninsula and cramped pantry transformed the kitchen into a more efficient space. The island was painted black to make it appear as though it were a found piece of furniture. One side of the island conceals a stool; drawers are on each of the long sides.

Tiles meant for flooring are used instead as a cooktop backsplash. Preassembled in 12-inch squares, they were then rearranged based on the homeowners' color and pattern preferences.

cooktop, for instance, features a center shelf that sports armoire-style doors that open outward and then slide back into the sides of the cabinet, revealing herbs and spices and cooking oils. "Having the shelf placed right there, with those doors, makes for very easy access," says Eileen. A lower shelf behind bifold doors holds the coffee pot and toaster, while the top cabinet, fitted with conventional hinged doors, contains sundries.

Eileen wanted the new kitchen to blend in with the rest of the house. She wanted the room to look timeless, as though it were original to the house. Rubbed-through finishes on the cabinets—a technique where the wood is hand-sanded to mimic wear—went a long way in bringing this idea to fruition. Just as important as color and texture, though, were the shape and materials of the cabinets. The fancifully carved openings that define the cabinets above the double sink echo the French Normandy architectural motifs that crop up throughout the house. The curve of the range hood is also something out of a country home in France, says McFadden, who stuccoed the flue to make it appear as part of the structure of the house rather than as an installed piece of cabinetry. Its carved corbels further amplify the comfortable French Country theme.

Now that the renovation is complete, the family can fully appreciate the new roominess of the kitchen. Thanks to well-defined work zones, they no longer get in each other's way. The prep area—the refrigerator and sink—is independent from the cleanup triangle—the double sink, dishwasher and dishes. This liberation is not unique to this remodel, but not everybody focuses on this when they renovate their kitchen. Separating these functions means nobody fights over the same corners of the room.

FAMILY-FRIENDLY DESIGN IDEAS

CLEAR PASSAGE Open archways and sliding doors—instead of doors that swing in and out—are less likely to get in the way when different family members are walking in different directions.

SITTING TALL Barstools at the center island are a convenient place for breakfast—or a chat with Mom while she prepares dinner.

REDUCE, REUSE A recycling separator ensures that even the kids can help keep cans and bottles under control.

SNACK CENTRAL Provide places for kids to put together their own munchies—a microwave oven with adjacent counter space can be placed in easy reach and out of the way of the cook.

LIGHT The best position in the house for a breakfast area is one that can receive an abundance of natural light. Nothing beats the sun for illuminating meals and reading material.

HOT WIRES If your kitchen will have a computer station, plan for cabling, phone lines, and electrical circuits before the renovation begins.

BEYOND THE BOX Take cabinets beyond the world of standard drawers and cupboards. Tailor to your family's exact needs with bins, tilt-out trays, spice drawers, pullout pantries, rollout cabinets, and unusually narrow, wide, short, or tall units.

PLEASANT PALETTE Light colors, warm woods, and good lighting make for a welcoming atmosphere that won't fatigue your family's eyes or senses over the years, as more dramatic treatments might.

DESIGN

A KIDS' SNACK ZONE, set away from the main traffic path, might have its own sink, along with an undercounter fridge and microwave. A plus: every one of those additions will come in handy for entertaining.

HAVING SEVERAL WORK AREAS with more than one—even more than two—sinks is key. Along with a kids' snack zone, it's helpful to have a crafts-and-homework zone, with storage for related supplies, away from the food-prep area.

A BREAKFAST NOOK with a built-in banquette is a favorite with kids. Put the children in charge of household recycling and help them by incorporating built-in recycling bins or pullouts somewhere in the traffic pattern near the back or garage door.

TRY FOR AN OPEN FLOOR PLAN with multiple ways in and out. A dead-end plan, such as a kitchen in a tight U shape, makes access difficult for more than one or two people.

MATERIALS AND APPLIANCES

A REFRIGERATOR WITH ICE AND WATER in the door encourages children to drink more water, but it's a convenience for everyone else in the household, too.

INTERNET ACCESS FROM THE KITCHEN is a good idea, especially as parents want to keep an eye on what their kids are doing online.

HAVING TWO DISHWASHERS makes sense for big families. Instead of standard models, dishwasher drawers are convenient; they operate independently, with each having about half the capacity of a standard dishwasher, and you can start one while still filling the other.

SOLID PAINTED CABINETS AREN'T USUALLY the best choices for heavy-use kitchens. Cabinets take a lot of wear and tear, so they must be durable—but they also have to look good. Wood cabinets are usually the best choice, but a solid painted finish is apt to show scuffs and kick marks, especially where stools are pulled up to a breakfast bar or counter. If you want painted cabinets, go for a glazed overfinish that gives the cabinetry a more aged look and helps conceal wear.

Forward into the past

MICHELLE AND PETER O'CONNER loved plenty of things about their 250-year-old Massachusetts farmhouse. The kitchen, however, wasn't one of them. A 1970s remodel stripped away much of its Colonial charm, leaving depressing dark-paneled cabinets and outdated appliances. Along with the typical old-house pitfalls, the couple faced the problem of incorporating modern amenities in a space unequipped to handle them. "The gaps between the floorboards were so large that you could see the basement underneath," says Michelle, who lived with the shortcomings for three years before deciding the only practical solution was to gut the space and start over.

After consulting with Cathy Stathopoulos, CKD, of B&G Cabinets in Newburyport, Massachusetts, the homeowners elected to update the room without altering its original footprint. To open up the space, which dates back to the mid 1800s, part of a wall between the kitchen and sunroom was removed and the floor plan reworked, resulting in a functional U-shaped layout and improved traffic flow.

Along with storage space, counter-height seating designed to facilitate quick meals and conversation was a top priority for the couple. "There was no place for our three kids to sit down and have something to eat," says Michelle. A custom-designed desk next to the stove provides a convenient spot for snacks or a surface for school projects. The unit is equipped with storage drawers and also functions as a message center.

From the start of the project, the O'Conners gravitated toward fixtures and finishes compatible with the rest of their Colonial home. A massive mid-19th-century pine hutch, one of their first purchases, anchors the 230-square-foot space and conceals modern appliances from view. Inspired by the antique piece, Michelle opted for custom maple cabinets with both open and closed storage to complement the eclectic farmhouse interior. "We wanted the cabinets to resemble freestanding furniture," she says. "I didn't want anything that looked too new."

Custom wood countertops crafted from reclaimed timber and an old-fashioned soapstone sink contribute to the nostalgic charm of the room. Unable

The custom Shaker-style maple cabinets were given a finish that simulates a time-worn look. Antique harvesting baskets corral small appliances. Wood countertops, crafted from 200-year-old hemlock, were glued together and then sealed with polyurethane.

ABOVE: Three young children in the house made a convenient snack area a priority. Equipped with pullout drawers, the space also functions as a message center and school-project area. A mix of open shelves and glass-fronted cabinets above it conveys farmhouse style.

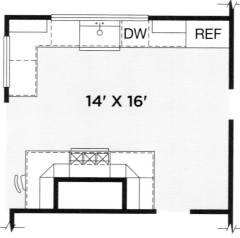

DW   REF

14' X 16'

OPPOSITE BELOW: A sleuthing expedition in nearby Gloucester yielded the antique pine cupboard, which cleverly conceals a bottled-water dispenser and microwave oven.

PASS-THROUGHS

IN HOMES WHERE TEARING DOWN A WALL between the kitchen and the family area isn't practical, either for structural reasons or because the wall provides precious storage space in a kitchen that's on the small side, pass-throughs are a fantastic way to achieve an open, welcoming look that will allow the homeowners to entertain often.

A pass-through is just what its name implies. It's an opening in the wall through which, ostensibly, food and dishes would be passed. In addition, it can serve the same function as so many of the multilevel islands shown in this book: Friends and well-wishers can gather and ogle the spread as it's being prepared. It also allows eyes to peer through in the opposite direction so that moms and dads can keep tabs on the goings-on in the household.

From a design standpoint, framing an opening is fairly straightforward; placing it is the tricky part. A pass-through does a lot more than allow efficient passage of chips and dip from kitchen to family room. Ideally, it will allow maximum exposure to the most possible areas, be they the front entry, the back porch, the hallway or stairwell.

In opening to other rooms, a pass-through can also achieve an indirect benefit. Because many of those adjacent rooms will have larger windows, that sunlight is likely to find its way into the kitchen via the pass-through.

Although a pass-through often links the kitchen and dining area, in many households, the hole in the wall not only offers visual benefits, it also allows for greater aural (read: verbal) communication. Like many

good design elements, the function of a pass-through evolves over time; a well-designed pass-through will lend itself to multiple uses and benefits as the family changes.

One such benefit is creating a sense of openness in a small kitchen. The foremost goal in such a space, of course, should be to create an efficient, functional kitchen with the right appliances, countertops, and cabinets, as discussed throughout this book. A pass-through, though, can add visual interest to a confined space. It introduces an element of surprise, teasing the eye with what lies beyond, and it clearly opens the kitchen to the next room.

The decision to add a pass-through depends on the mind-set of the homeowner. Some people feel constrained by small kitchens and want to stretch out, and some are more comfortable in such cozy confines. A pass-through offers both functionality and pleasing aesthetics for the former group.

PASS-THROUGH POINTERS

FRAME AND FOCUS Consider the pass-through an "interior window." Even though a pass-through opens only into another interior space, visually it acts as a window by letting in additional light and relieving the cramped feel of a small room. It also frames a view, so think about what you want to obscure as well as what you want to open up. Some people may not want their kitchen sink visible from the dining room table.

ARCHITECTURAL ACCENT Make use of the opportunity for drama and surprise. Any opening prompts curiosity; visitors to your kitchen will be drawn to the pass-through as though it were a window. With this in mind, consider enhancing the pass-through with eye-catching elements, like a subtle arch.

FUNCTION JUNCTION Locate the pass-through where it will serve multiple purposes. Pass-throughs link public areas in your home, so serving communication as well as food should be a goal.

LOOK BEYOND THE BOX If a pass-through can be positioned not just for utility but to frame a view, so much the better. In one instance, a kitchen was at the back of the house, but the pass-through was placed to capture a river view through the front windows, 21 feet away.

TO SEE OR NOT TO SEE Fitting the pass-through with opaque shutters lets you muffle noise and hide views of a messy kitchen, but the panels will also cut off light. If the pass-through is important for brightening the kitchen, consider translucent or transparent shutters, or omit them altogether.

FRAME THE VIEW Before cutting into the wall, think about how much space there will be between the bottom of the pass-through and the counter behind it. In the kitchen mentioned above (the one with the river view), the owner says there's only one thing she would change about her new kitchen: She purchased a sculptural faucet for the main sink without considering the pass-through. She loves the faucet but wishes it weren't visible through the opening.

INTERIOR WINDOWS

The design and natural-wood finish of these kitchen pass-throughs were influenced by the windows on the opposite walls of the rooms. Glass panes keep the kitchen visually connected to the rest of the ground floor, even when the panels are closed. Though some prefer the unfettered access a framed opening provides, being able to seal off the space—either with hinged panels, a pull-down tambour, or a mini–pocket door—can prove to be a boon in busy households.

Colonial compact

PAM AND GEORGE ZAISER CONVERTED a walkout basement into an 1,100-square-foot apartment for Pam's mother, but in so doing, they deliberately tried to keep the 21st century at bay. The Pennsylvania homeowners preferred the look of a Colonial farmhouse—a style Pam's mother knew from her prior residence—but were concerned that modern appliances and amenities might detract from its charm. "I didn't want a big refrigerator sticking out," admits Pam, who played an active role in the design project. "I wanted the room to function like a kitchen, but without it obviously looking like one."

They turned to Roy McLain, CMKBD, of Advanced Kitchens and Bath in Mechanicsburg, Pennsylvania. His challenge was to design a functional, accessible kitchen in a small area. His first decision was to install framing timbers overhead. The beams were vintage lumber the couple snapped up for a song after spotting an ad in a local paper. Random-width pine flooring went down in the kitchen and family room for a seamless transition between spaces. Then came pale, solid-maple butcher block countertops to complement the rough-hewn timbers and visually lighten the 8x11-foot space.

Instead of all cabinets sitting flush to the floor and reaching to the ceiling, the owners opted for some custom cabinets with feet at the bottom and beaded inset panels that mimic freestanding furniture. On one wall, a hutch with a distressed finish holds a farmhouse sink with deep apron front. As Pam's mother is right-handed, the sink sits to the left of the dishwasher to make rinsing, loading, and unloading easier. Above the basin, a plate rack showcases colorful crockery. Another hutchlike piece sits opposite, outfitted with an undercounter refrigerator, a concealed microwave, and plenty of drawers—some of them open-topped sliding baskets—and cabinets.

In lieu of a range is a cooking alcove, with a two-burner cooktop and conventional oven, which anchors the work triangle and creates a focal point at the end of the room. On either side of the oven, pullout storage drawers provide easy access to pots, pans, and pantry items. Hand-painted Italian tiles of artists and musicians at play punctuate the primarily all-white backsplash and provide whimsy.

Simple wooden knobs and thumb latches (called "dog's ears" in Colonial times) impart period flavor. An uncomplicated Colonial palette of milky blue and mustard-yellow unifies the tiny space without overpowering it.

ABOVE: The two-burner cooktop and oven in this small cooking alcove are reminiscent of an old-fashioned hearth.

OPPOSITE: Two brand-new plumbing products hark back a couple of centuries, as a farmhouse sink with a deep apron meets an elegant high-arc faucet in hand-rubbed bronze finish. The hutch they're in also serves as a cleanup area.

ABOVE: Along with a collection of antiques and solid pine flooring, vintage beams and period-inspired cabinets capture the essence of farmhouse charm.

OPPOSITE, BELOW: For a functional kitchen with a period look, the dishwasher, along with other appliances, was hidden behind custom cabinet panels.

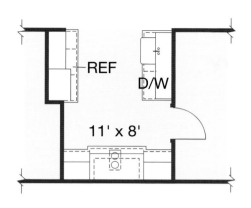

REF

D/W

11' x 8'

ABOVE: The U-shaped layout opens directly into the family room. For ease and efficiency, the designer configured a tight work triangle, placing major appliances within a few steps of each other.

RIGHT: A compact, undercounter refrigerator—just fine for the space's single user—leaves more room for drawers and cabinets.

COUNTRY SECRETS

DECORATIVE STORAGE Built-in plate rack and cup hooks convey period charm and display kitchen crockery.

COUNTRY COLOR SCHEME Colonial colors of milky blue and mustard-yellow reinforce the period look.

AUTHENTIC MATERIALS Exposed beams, recycled-wood floor, and vintage-inspired cabinets capture the farmhouse look.

CLEVER COOKTOP A cooking alcove replaces the traditional hearth and improves the efficiency of the range hood.

LIGHTING A reproduction punched-tin light fixture mimics earlier period lighting and provides ample overhead illumination. Low-voltage undercabinet halogen lights provide task lighting for kitchen chores.

HISTORICAL HARDWARE Turned knobs and thumb latches replicate the look of Colonial-era hardware and allow cabinets to open and close easily.

UNDERCOVER APPLIANCES Panel doors conceal major appliances. Custom flush-toe cabinets imitate the look of freestanding furniture.

30 WAYS TO UPGRADE YOUR KITCHEN ON A BUDGET

SIMPLE ALTERATIONS CAN ADD NEW LIFE and appeal to a kitchen without the hassle of a major remodel. Paint, wallpaper, trims, tiles, updated accessories, and other interesting accents can provide instant upgrades for weary and dated spaces. Read on for more easy ideas!

- Update your cabinets with glass insert panels—clear, textured, or stained glass—on the doors.
- Using textiles or pottery for inspiration, paint unglazed tiles for a backsplash, then have them fired at a DIY ceramic center.
- Cover an unattractive floor with self-adhesive vinyl tiles.
- Spruce up cabinet surfaces by stripping them and changing to a lighter or darker finish. Refinishing is easier and less messy than ever with new stripping products. (The first cabinet may be a challenge, but skill level increases rapidly.)
- Change accessories at a whim: floor runners, chair cushions, simple valances, and table linens.

- Add molding to give the room architectural interest.
- Redo window treatments in luscious colors. It can be as easy as clipping linen napkins to a curtain rod.
- Replace hardware. Porcelain knobs, figurine handles, or vintage-style metal pulls give new life and a coordinated look to cabinetry.
- Panel the doors of existing cabinets. (Adding molding strips creates the illusion of paneling to flat surfaces.) Then paint them to freshen the look of the kitchen.
- Renew a tired pot rack with a coat of shimmery metallic paint.
- Install small lights inside glass-fronted cabinets to better display colorful collectibles.
- Update the look of a sink with a stylish new faucet and accessories.
- Mount a single open shelf under cabinets to hold mugs, cereal bowls, and other everyday dishes.
- Hang up Peg-Board painted in jaunty colors. Ensure that items are returned to their rightful place by painting outline shadows.
- Turn an old table into a useful island. To enhance the top, cover the surface with a marble or granite slab or butcher block.
- Use letter transfers to spell out favorite foods or to record a traditional family dish on a kitchen wall.
- Cut a piece of oilcloth to fit the floor area near the sink. Paint it to match window treatments or patterned china, perhaps. Polyurethane the oilcloth for durability.

Hanging a pot rack from the ceiling not only expands storage space, it also adds visual interest to the upper register of the room.

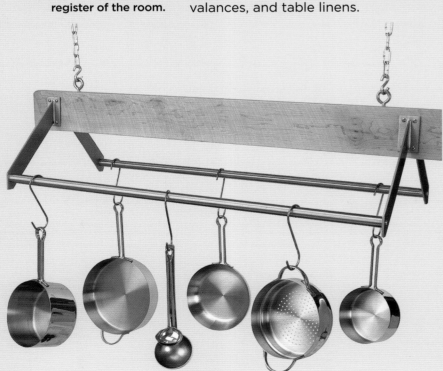

Log-term commitment

JENNIFER AND ACE LANE AREN'T THE TYPE who would surrender their Colorado cabin to strangers. Compelling circumstances arose, however, when workers armed with chain saws showed up at their doorstep. It was officially time for their kitchen remodel, and they quickly packed up and left town. "We knew it was going to be an involved process," says Jennifer.

After a decade of hard use, most of the light-colored surfaces in the Lanes' old kitchen had succumbed to stains, scratches, and scuff marks. "We basically wore the place out," says the busy mom and only female in a household that includes three boys—ages 5, 7, and 11—and two golden retrievers, to boot. To avoid having to remodel again in another 10 years, Jennifer and her husband, owners of a 180-acre tree farm and landscaping company located 20 miles north of Aspen, sought professional advice from Dan Ellis, CKD.

By its nature, a log home poses particular challenges. Unlike conventional frame construction, once log walls are in place, moving or eliminating any of them compromises the structural integrity of the building. So the primary concern was creating more space in the existing kitchen without moving walls or enlarging the footprint in any way.

At the top of the Lanes' wish list was a bigger and better-equipped island with convenient pull-up seating. "We needed a place for the kids to eat," says Jennifer. Additional storage and shelf space, too, were obvious priorities, as the boys' appetites were due for steady increases. They also wanted to swap a bulky side-by-side refrigerator for space-saving, larger-capacity models.

The designer finessed a seemingly inflexible floor plan, enlarging a pass-through and appropriating space from an unused corner of the living room, in order to create a small butler's pantry. Squeezing out space for the island proved more difficult, however.

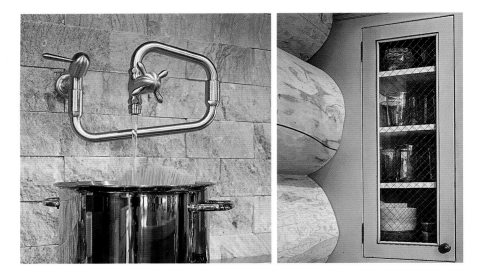

With further expansion no longer an option, he used a chain saw to trim 6 inches from walls, eliminating gaps between logs and creating a smoothly planed surface to give cabinets a recessed appearance. The radical move netted an extra 2 feet of floor space—enough for the island and, really, the only way the island could fit.

The owners ultimately settled on a simple raised-panel cabinet design with beadboard insets and bracket feet.

To keep the cabinets from disappearing into the log work, Ellis suggested using an antique green finish, reminiscent of split-pea soup, for the cabinets on the perimeter walls and in the pantry.

The reworked floor plan is an L shape with a tight work triangle. Although the total area of the kitchen increased by only 40 square feet, the space bursts with amenities, including two slim refrigerators, refrigerated drawers, a built-in microwave, a stainless steel commercial-style range, two sinks, a dishwasher, a trash disposal, and a recycling center. Abundant natural materials, such as native Colorado timber, reclaimed oak, copper, and rough-hewn stone were incorporated throughout, imparting a rich visual texture to the room and echoing the rugged terrain outside. Rejecting the pale woods selected the first time around, Jennifer insisted on darker "kid-friendly" colors and "indestructible" finishes that could stand up to the demands of an active family.

As a result of careful planning, the remodeled kitchen fulfills its function as the hub of family activities. In addition, although the room appears to have evolved over a long period of time, the renovation took a couple of months. During the worst of the construction, after the chain saws showed up, the family decamped to Hawaii, a solution Jennifer recommends. "When we came back, everything looked a lot better!"

DW REF

13' X 14'6"

REF

HOW TO CHOOSE CABINETS

Because quality cabinets can easily eat up 40 percent of a remodeling budget, choosing wisely can be among the most nerve-racking decisions a homeowner faces. Too often, remodelers jump the gun, committing to a particular brand or style before locking in a floor plan or appliances. To make things easier, it helps to remember that cabinet styles generally fall into one of two major categories. Recessed or raised-panel doors indicate traditional styling. Flush-mounted doors are compatible with more contemporary environments.

To complement the rustic beauty and character of their log home, Jennifer and Ace Lane selected traditional raised-panel cabinets. To avoid anything too trendy, their designer suggested using an antique-green finish to keep the cabinets from getting lost in all the unfinished wood of the walls. Although the homeowners could have opted for a contemporary style, the familiar beadboard detailing and furniture-like style recall the past and capture the warmth and ambience of their log home.

The counters are made of nonporous, heat-resistant soapstone, which, over time, will darken to a charcoal-gray. Random-plank flooring made from reclaimed oak is already distressed and can stand up to scuff marks and skateboards.

A contemporary aesthetic, squared

Defining the island and adding an element of contrast to the ceiling, an overhead panel of maple-veneered plywood also acts as a foil for lighting fixtures.

A MOST UNLIKELY SOURCE, A TABLE, became the springboard of inspiration for the design of this Toronto-area kitchen. Homeowners Kathy Crozier and Bill Wong love their table, with its maple legs and etched-glass top accented with squares of clear glass. Those squares became the defining element throughout the kitchen, designed by Robin Siegerman, CKD, of Sieguzi Interior Designs.

Kathy and Bill have a contemporary sensibility, which became a tremendous asset in conjuring a design for a 1985 house with no strong architectural details. In this regard, Siegerman lucked out; the owners' design sense gave her license to fulfill their vision.

Tiles of Brazilian slate that cover the floor and one wall form the foundation of a square-grid motif that repeats time and time again in the kitchen. Throughout the room, more squares pop up in details large and small: in cabinets with glass doors textured with crosshatching, in 1-inch mosaic tiles that form the backsplashes, and in the dissolving checkerboard of the dining-area windows. Rather than trying to hide the joints in the maple paneling surrounding the windows, Siegerman turned the seams into a subtle right-angled reveal. Even the chairs and light sconces give testimony to squares.

But unrelieved 90-degree angles are far from the whole story of the kitchen. The room itself is not rectangular; a slate-covered fireplace wall clips off one corner. Moreover, the predominant features of the space are its irregularly shaped island and the ceiling canopy that exactly mirrors the odd shape. Kathy and Bill knew they wanted something more interesting than a big, square island, according to Siegerman. They also wanted some visual interest on the ceiling, as the kitchen, at more than 20x15 feet, felt a bit barnlike to begin with. In addition to its visual grace, the canopy provides light through a mixture of canister and pendant lights. Also, its swath of maple veneer lowers the ceiling in the center of the room, defining a warmer, more intimate space. Adding to that cozy feeling is the built-in desk area, whose trapezoidal work surface adds inches as well as interest to the niche.

The sophisticated contemporary aesthetic so critically important to Sieg-

erman's clients did not come at the expense of practicality. After all, this is a hardworking kitchen for a family that includes three sons, ages 9, 17, and 21. The high-gloss maple-patterned laminate cabinets are, says the designer, more durable and easier to maintain than wood. The island counter combines concrete and stainless steel for beauty and ruggedness. Stainless steel appliances, including a built-in coffeemaker and an under-counter wine cooler, complete the up-to-the-moment look.

In the end, how successful is the design? Given the generous floor space, ample counters, and multiple work areas, everyone manages to stay out of one another's way. And, in the ultimate affirmation, Kathy and Bill claim they don't go into the living room anymore.

MATERIAL MATTERS
THE BRAZILIAN SLATE that covers the floor and one wall can be used in a traditional or contemporary interior. It brings warmth to the room, but it's also clean looking.
GLASS MOSAIC TILES used for the backsplash have a luminous quality. Unlike ceramic, glass has depth and translucency; the eye doesn't stop at the surface.
THE LLUMAR FILM on the dining-area windows is often used in commercial applications. Durable and scratch resistant but ultrathin, the film is cut into precise patterns that are applied to the glass to achieve an effect resembling etching, but at a much lower cost.

ABOVE: In the dining area, squares appear in the lights, chairs, and windows.

OPPOSITE BELOW LEFT: Tucked into a corner of the kitchen, the range adds a lively diagonal line to the room. The countertops that bookend the appliance are heat-resistant concrete.

21' X 17'

MW

REF

ABOVE: Well-defined workstations and a spacious floor plan make the kitchen a real comfort to work in.

ABOVE: Just to the left of the refrigerator, an LCD television flips down from beneath the microwave cabinet. Homeowner Bill Wong is a fan of the TV: "It's thin and space saving, and it has a nice, bright picture."

ABOVE: Angling the front of the desk out beyond the standard depth of the cabinets adds needed area to its work surface.

ABOVE: In the backsplash, aqua, teal, and steel-gray glass tiles echo the hues of the slate, concrete, and stainless steel used in the kitchen.

Split-level personality

AFTER FIVE YEARS IN THEIR SPLIT-LEVEL BRICK HOME in Arlington, Virginia, Sheri Winter and husband Mark Duros decided it was time to update their 11x11-foot kitchen. "The room didn't flow well, and it lacked storage area," recalls Sheri. "We knew we were not making good use of the space we had." Sheri was interested in displaying her collection of egg cups, colorful pottery, and pig-themed cookie jars, but Mark seemed more into researching appliances on the Internet and coming up with his own list of must-haves for the new space. They both hoped to create a comfortable eat-in kitchen with abundant storage.

The young couple interviewed a number of designers before deciding to work with Mary Maier Galloway, CKD, and carpenter Stuart Willems. Maier Galloway remembers the old kitchen as being pretty generic, with all the spaces pretty much thrown together. She spoke with Sheri and Mark to get a feel for what they expected. The couple wanted the kitchen to remain the same size and stay in the same location—between the dining and living rooms. Working within these guidelines, Maier Galloway came up with a design that improved both the function and look of the kitchen.

One of the first major decisions of the project was cabinet selection. The couple chose attractive maple cabinets with a vanilla-bean painted finish and satin-nickel pulls. They were shooting for something with a warm, homey feeling, but the cabinets also had to fit in with their refrigerator and cooktop. Some of the new cabinets feature glass fronts to display Sheri's collectibles; a shallow built-in shelf was created just for her egg cups.

The next important change was replacing the worn vinyl floor with oak strips. The new hardwood floor adds a sense of richness to the space, as well as historical continuity. Such a treatment would have been typical when the home was built, and several

other rooms in the house also have wood floors. So it only made sense to continue that theme into the kitchen.

The Softstone countertops in a sage-green/tea-leaf-beige color resist stains and can stand up to hot pots from the stove. "We knew we wanted a solid surface for the counters, but with a warm look," says Sheri.

The new countertops balance with the stainless steel appliances, including a refrigerator, smooth-glass cooktop with slim pull-out hood, and a handy microwave/convection oven combo unit. Since the busy couple rarely bake, they decided to forgo a traditional radiant oven. The designer fought them on this idea, fearing what might happen if they decided to sell the house. Wisely, she left room in the surrounding cabinets to accommodate a full-size oven if they change their minds, or if they sell the home and the new owners want to install one. A dishwasher to the right of the sink makes cleaning up a simple process. Its entire front is a custom cabinet panel, so it looks like all the other cabinets and doesn't spoil the old-fashioned atmosphere.

No attention to detail was spared in this project, including the lighting. In addition to a fun retro fixture in the middle of the ceiling, there are undercabinet halogen lights on dimmers for the task areas and recessed lights over the sink and the inviting banquette. The glass-front display cabinets also have lighting inside, so their contents stand out when guests stop by at night.

A toasty pumpkin color covers the walls and is the final touch that helps pull together the look of this spirited space. The sum of all of this, as the designer notes, is a kitchen remodel that showcases how it is possible to make a space beautiful and functional, and still have fun and imbue it with the owners' distinct personalities.

CUSTOM BANQUETTE

With a built-in bench on one side and two chairs on the other, Sheri and Mark were able to create an ideal spot to grab a quick meal. "We wanted a place to relax and hang out in the kitchen and use that dead space in the corner," explains Sheri. Mary Maier Galloway custom-designed the bench and table following some drawings that Mark found in an old book on bungalows.
The freestanding table with maple top rests against a display cabinet that gives the couple an attractive way to show off their collectibles. The table legs were painted the same warm vanilla-bean color used for the new cabinets. The chairs grouped with the banquette were found at a flea market. They were painted, and upholstered for comfort. This banquette is a wonderful example of how this couple and designer used every inch of available space in this major kitchen remodel.

With the help of a false door-and-drawer front panel, the dishwasher goes undercover.

WORKING WALLS

In a small kitchen, wall space can't be wasted. Sheri Winter's collection of colorful ceramic pig jars are proudly displayed in built-in glass-fronted cabinets, while whimsical egg cups are neatly arrayed in a custom-designed shelf. A wall telephone conserves counter space while helping to evoke the era.

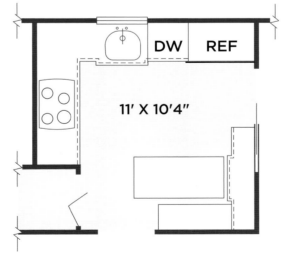

LEFT: Keeping within the footprint of the existing room, designer Mary Maier Galloway coalesced disjointed work areas throughout the kitchen to fit the homeowners' cooking habits.

11' X 10'4"

DW | REF

LEFT: Boasting counter space on both sides of the glass cooktop, the kitchen provides the couple with plenty of room to prepare meals.

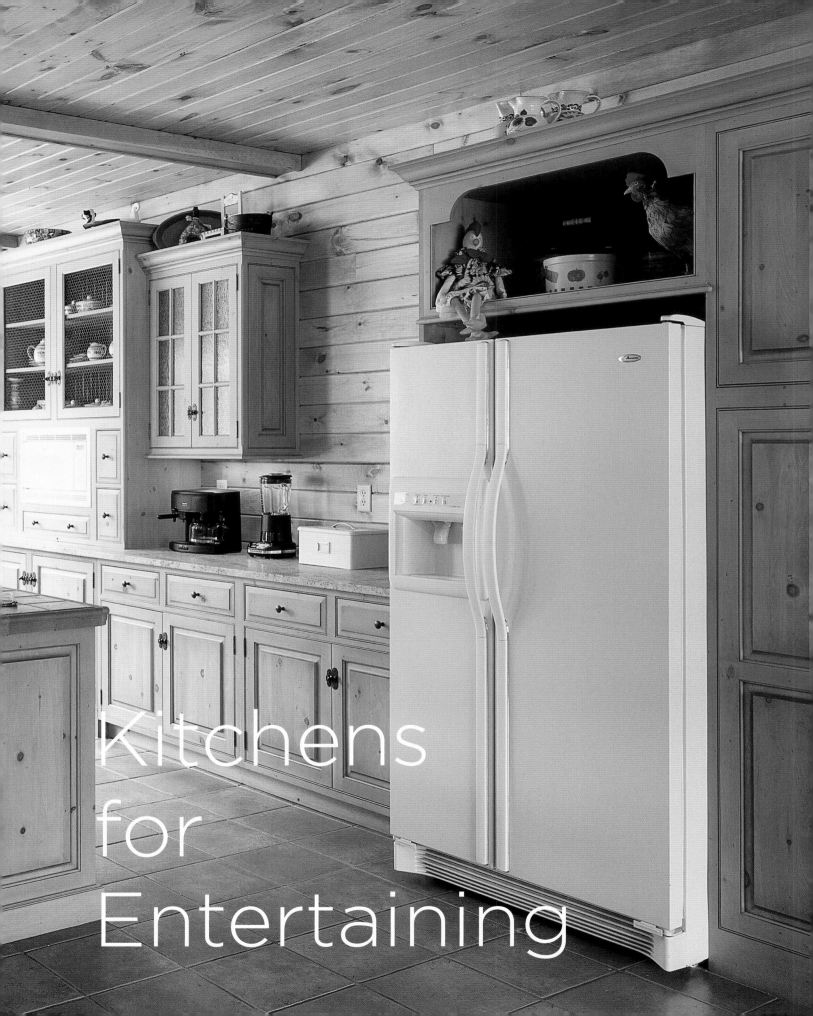

Kitchens
for
Entertaining

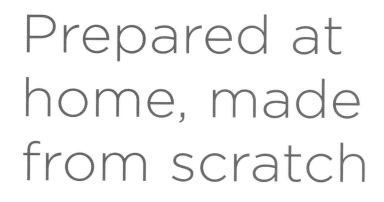

Prepared at home, made from scratch

BUILDING NEW HOMES IS LIKE BAKING COOKIES. The results can be whatever their creators want them to be. Suzanne and Mark Birnbaum poured some specific ingredients into their new Craftsman-style home overlooking a golf course outside Saginaw, Michigan. They ended up with a family kitchen and a transformed first floor all set for entertaining.

"I needed a space that would make it easy for me to prepare dinner in a hurry," says Suzanne. "Our daughters both have basketball practice in the evenings, plus we have season tickets to two hockey teams and attend a lot of high school and junior high school sports. Basically, the kids come home, we make dinner, we eat dinner, and we are back out the door again."

To accommodate their schedule, the Birnbaums hired designer Bernard Maday, CKD, to create an open, efficient space that would make preparing food and catching quick snacks a snap. They also wanted a gracious, welcoming kitchen that flowed easily into nearby rooms. The result of Maday's effort is a large, comfortable space that connects the entire ground floor of the Birnbaums' house, both functionally and visually. All of the living areas get daily use, but the kitchen is hands down the center of family life.

No wonder. Thanks to careful planning and thoughtful choices, the kitchen is easy to work in and easy on the eyes. Maday incorporated a practical, extra-large stove and refrigerator, plus a trash compactor, recycling center, two sinks with disposers, and plenty of counters and storage space—but still managed to make sure the space looked homey. The floors are a warm, honey-toned wood, the cabinets look like furniture, and the smaller appliances are either

hidden altogether or masked by panels that match the furniture-look cabinets.

Suzanne likes the casual farmhouse decor but disdains clutter on the counters, so she needs lots of storage. Maday fulfilled that need generously. The kitchen is a whopping 500 square feet—big enough for not one but two islands. Ten-foot ceilings offer tons of cupboard room in the kitchen. The walls have extra-high hanging cabinets, holding not only all the plates, pots, and dishes, but also appliances. A sturdy hidden shelf even allows Suzanne to keep her mixer on constant standby for cake baking. It swings up out of a base cabinet and locks securely into place whenever she and the girls want to whip up a batch of brownies for their sports teams' frequent bake sales.

With all that baking, cooking, and snacking, the dish load is often too much for one dishwasher, so Maday installed two: one for just-used dishes while the other is in operation. That kind of family-friendly practicality, combined with Maday's more than 30 years of experience designing kitchens and Suzanne's cozy-chic taste, resulted in an open-plan space that functions as "Birnbaum Family Central" from breakfast through the end of the evening news.

BRINGING THE OUTDOORS INSIDE

• Turn a windowsill into an herb garden with pots of basil, rosemary, mint, and sage.

• Force seasonally appropriate bulbs—such as grape hyacinth, daffodils, and tulips—to bloom indoors in spring for an early burst of color. Try wood sorrel or meadow saffron in summer, autumn crocus in fall, and paperwhite narcissus and amaryllis in winter—for scent and visual sensation.

• Make place mats and napkins of fabric imprinted with images of vintage garden implements.

• Turn the sunny corner of your kitchen into a conservatory with hanging pots of ivy and masses of flowering plants.

• Sew a fabulous valance of French Country toile for the window.

• Festoon a pot rack with garlands of braided garlic.

• Perch a ceramic rooster or hen on top of your kitchen cabinets.

• Indulge in essential oil soaps and cleaning collections with fragrances like lemon verbena, rosemary, mint, and lavender.

• Hang hand-painted salad plates or an asparagus platter on the wall.

• Embed strands of ivy in sphagnum moss to create an eye-catching wreath centerpiece for the kitchen table.

• Enjoy the long-lasting beauty of a Capodimonte porcelain fruit basket or a collection of hand-blown glass fruits.

• Show off individual blooms in old laboratory beakers.

• Set the table with bamboo or olive wood–handled cutlery.

• Add a touch of citrus to the kitchen with lemon plates.

ABOVE AND OPPOSITE ABOVE: Almost 40 feet of granite counters and two sinks offer lots of room for dinner prep—and flowers.

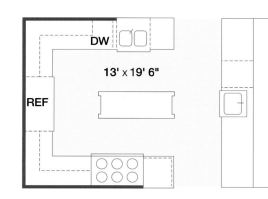

Welcoming the congregation

AFTER 21 YEARS IN THE BUSINESS, designer Jacqueline Balint, CKD, knows what her clients want even if they can't express their wishes so clearly. What she's learned is that no matter how hard hosts may try to get guests to enjoy snacks and entertainment in another room while they cook, those guests are going to congregate in the kitchen. So the cooks want kitchens where the guests can hang out but not be in the way. In this Southern California house, the designer tackles that common dilemma.

When Tim Keenan, an insurance executive with a 12-year-old son, Brian, remodeled his one-story 1952 tract house into a two-story Craftsman home, he was determined that every room reflect the vigorous style that flourished in the early part of the 20th century. "I like the look because it's masculine and classic," Tim says, "and it makes use of natural materials." Balint, too, appreciates Craftsman, a down-to-earth reaction to the fussy excesses of turn-of-the-century Victorian architecture, which was a hotbed of fanciful decorations and embellishments. The Craftsman school, on the other hand, embodies the opposite of clutter. It emphasizes the aesthetic of humble materials—the grains of woods, the patina of metals, the coloring of stone—as well as a high standard of workmanship.

Although the kitchen is a well-defined room, it is actually part of a casual suite of spaces that includes a dining area with a built-in hutch and a cozy nook with a fireplace. The floor plan allows for easy movement between these spaces, and this integration of rooms is the crowning touch of the design.

Tim and Brian often eat their breakfast at the bi-level island, which delineates the kitchen proper from the dining area. It also works to conceal the cooktop from guests. (The kitchen is in full view of the entry.) Indeed, other major appliances have gone

PRECEDING PAGES: Finely wrought cherry cabinets and chairs, leaded-glass lighting, and subtly hued countertops are all hallmarks of California Craftsman design.

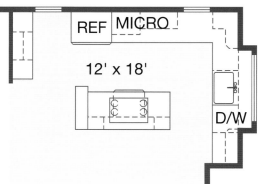

REF MICRO

12' x 18'

D/W

ABOVE: When paneled in wood, even an island-style vent hood assumes a Craftsman aesthetic.

LEFT: The open plan means the kitchen never has too many cooks.

CRAFTSMAN DETAILS MEET MODERN CONVENIENCE

RANGE HOOD Sheathed in cherry to match the cabinets, the hood cleans the air and complements its style. Halogen lights in the hood illuminate the cooktop.

LIGHT FIXTURES Choosing a family of fixtures for the pendant light, sconces, and chandelier gives a coordinated look to the flowing space without becoming visually repetitive.

TILE STYLE On the backsplash, squares of tumbled marble are placed on the diagonal, easing the grid of the cabinets.

CONTINUITY OF MATERIALS Using the same limestone of the countertops in the design of the hearth links the two areas together. Copper accent tiles do the same.

FIREPLACE AS FOCAL POINT Visible from the kitchen and central to the dining room, the fireplace becomes a center of attention and activity.

GLASS-FRONT CABINET DOORS Rendered in leaded glass—a classic Craftsman expression—these provide a bit of visual relief from the expanse of wood panel doors.

RESPONSIVE STORAGE Open shelving units neatly end wall-cabinet runs. Pantry storage is maximized with slide-out trays.

BUILT-IN BONUS A niche in the wall proved the ideal spot for a custom-designed, built-in hutch.

CONCEALED APPLIANCES Hiding the dishwasher and refrigerator behind cherry panels keeps the kitchen true to its historical style.

undercover as well, including the dishwasher and refrigerator, which are paneled in cherry to blend in with the kitchen cabinets.

The range hood, also encased in cherry, has the presence of a piece of furniture, its simple wood banding echoing the cabinet design. Given the high heat output of the range, Balint knew that a downdraft vent was not an option. Furthermore, she knew that exhaust hoods can be a design asset in their own right for the very reason that they can be coordinated with just about any kind of cabinet.

Architectural elements, design details, and materials also work to link the spaces together visually. Green limestone was chosen for countertops, both for how its muted color sets off the warm tones of the wood and for its matte finish. "A shiny surface would have ruined the look and mood of this kitchen," says Balint. The same stone appears again in the fireplace surround.

The kitchen is designed as part of a suite of three spaces, also consisting of a dining area and a nook for the fireplace, which is visible from the kitchen and is often a center of activity.

With its basic design premise of naturalness and simplicity, and a strong spirit of communality, it's no surprise that this well-crafted kitchen attracts both family and friends.

ABOVE: The dining area also includes a custom hutch built into a niche.

LEFT: Countertop nooks are great for small appliances. The next-door pantry has slide-out shelves so that even items in the back are reachable.

OPPOSITE: The bi-level island separates the kitchen from the dining area and hides the messy cooktop from guests.

Knot ready for prime time

BRIMMING WITH KNOTTY PINE, the spacious, well-designed kitchen of this contemporary barn-style home reflects the sociable lifestyle of its owner, a busy New York restaurateur who enjoys hosting friends and clanging ladles with culinary chums on weekends throughout the year. Working closely with Siobhan Daggett-Terenzi, of The Kitchen Factor in East Haven, Connecticut, the homeowner sought to create a space fit for a crowd. Befitting a person who hangs out with all those hyper-intense foodies, the homeowner has huge entertaining needs. Therefore, the designer had to make sure that a dozen or more people could work in the space without knocking elbows.

The volume of cooks notwithstanding, uncomplicated entertaining was the principal objective, and thus the 300-square-foot open plan is an efficient U-shaped layout. Designated zones handle food prep, cooking, and cleanup chores. A six-burner commercial range replaces the traditional hearth, accommodating both professional and neophyte chefs. The range serves as a focal point, adding both drama and function.

Rustic yet refined, the room percolates with clean lines and carefully considered details. Throughout the space is a great deal of pine, but through fastidious planning, subtle variations in the finish prevent the wood from overpowering the interior. Another challenge was trying to break up the horizontal planes of the space to keep it from becoming monotonous.

To punch up the palette, the designer introduced a robust shade of dark green. This color was such a huge hit with the client, it showed up again—as an accent to distinguish the cabinets from the pine walls and ceilings—in such key pieces as a wall-mounted hutch, a sink base, and pullout storage drawers. Such variations in colors and finishes contribute to the overall personality of the

room, making it appear as though each element evolved over time. This was certainly the desired effect, as nobody wanted the room to look as if it had just been built. To make sure all the finishes jibed with each other, the designer worked closely with both the cabinet manufacturer and the builder to select appropriate colors and stains. The homeowner chose white appliances and a deep-green range (there's that color again) that underscores the casual, unstudied design while visually tying the space together.

Expansive windows along the southeastern wall frame the ever-changing views of the Connecticut countryside. A double apron sink and a pair of dishwashers make for easy cleanup and accommodate a tribe of cooks. A large island functions as both a pantry and a prep area. Equipped with a second sink and deep drawers, it provides an additional work site, allowing guests to grab a knife (or any other suitable tool) and participate in culinary chores—a prerequisite to dining in this house. Even the designer knows that any visitor who isn't working isn't part of the party, and everyone who shows up gets an assignment.

Although pine rather obviously dominates the space, the design includes plenty of other natural materials and finishes. Slabs of granite comprise the counters, providing the easy maintenance associated

PRECEDING PAGES: The pine-paneled walls and ceiling impart visual warmth and keep the space from feeling cavernous. Providing actual warmth for chilly Connecticut winters, radiant heating lies beneath the tile floor.

ABOVE: Base cabinets with rollout trays hold baskets of seasonal fruit and vegetables. Pullout waste and recycling is in the cabinet next to the sink.

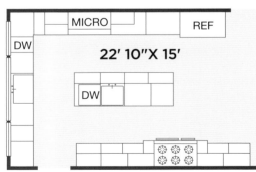

ABOVE: The relaxing atmosphere and rustic charm of the kitchen make it a magnet for company. The 300-square-foot room can accommodate a crowd of 20. The overflow guests, if any, can mingle in an adjoining dining area.

HANDCRAFTED CABINETS

Cabinets are a critical visual factor in designing a kitchen. They determine the character of the room. Traditional wooden cabinets establish the cozy ambience typical of a country kitchen, and a mix of slightly mismatched pieces can produce an authentic look.

ABOVE: The Shaker-style cabinetry shown here has a combination of finishes with several decorative enhancements, such as stacked molding, fretwork frieze detailing, beadboard paneling, mullion doors with glass inserts, and a dish-rack cabinet.

BELOW: This cabinet with drawers sits atop counters and contributes a custom hutch look.

ABOVE: Dark green relieves the expanse of pine in several areas of the kitchen. This painted hutch has chicken-wire inserts and a painted beadboard back.

Equipped with a prep sink and second dishwasher, the 9x3½-foot island is designed for multiple cooks. Pullout storage drawers on both sides provide ready access to items needed for meal preparation.

with this natural stone; the backsplash incorporates tumbled marble with incised diamonds. The work island features a countertop of 6-inch-square ceramic tiles in a warm terra-cotta, reinforcing the owner's preference for earthy, organic hues and textures. The faucet on the island does the same with a homey, rustic copper finish.

In a room this size, symmetry plays an important role. The homeowner and designer paid a great deal of attention to the placement of cabinets and appliances. A custom-crafted storage unit, flanked by twin glass-fronted cabinets, is perfectly positioned between two overhead beams. Directly opposite is a hutch, also with visible contents, even though in this case the see-through material is chicken wire.

Although designed to serve the needs of a professional cook, the space elicits compliments from everyone who uses it. The designer, who, as an occasional guest, has witnessed its workings firsthand, says this major production is not just for show: It's a real-life kitchen that welcomes both family and friends to come in and get involved in the action.

LEFT: The walls, ceiling, and cabinets are all about pine, but subtle variations in finishes keep the space from becoming boring. The raised-panel cabinetry features beaded inset doors stained with a brown glaze that has been slightly distressed to give an aged appearance.

ABOVE: The six-burner range has a griddle. The depth of the wall cabinets was increased from the standard 12 to 13 inches so that oversize platters and large serving dishes could fit inside them.

RIGHT: A wall of windows looks down on the bucolic countryside of rolling pastures and woodlands. The nice view, a double-basin farmer's sink and two dishwashers make heavy cleanup easier to tolerate.

38 WAYS TO WARM UP YOUR KITCHEN

WHEN PEOPLE ENTER YOUR KITCHEN—be they family, friends, or perfect strangers—they should feel welcome. They should smile. If your kitchen seems a little cold, a little generic, the following list of suggestions will surely offer a springboard of ideas to help exorcise the drabs from the room.

Warm up the kitchen by making a welcoming tableau with a hand-painted sign and a vase of fresh-cut flowers.

• Keep a brimming bowl of fruit on the table or a full cookie jar on the counter to welcome visitors.
• Sew cushions for chairs or counter stools to encourage guests to linger.
• Paint the walls in creamy tones.

• Add warmth with colorful ceramics or whimsical accessories.
• Introduce fabric, such as rugs or valances, for a softening effect.
• Drape a tabletop with runners.
• Display pottery on open shelves.
• Celebrate with seasonal accents like wreaths, swags, or collectibles.
• Add texture with a weathered farmhouse table.
• Grow herbs in containers to scent the air—and season the meals you prepare for guests.
• Adjust lighting to include soft, ambient light for entertaining and clear light for cooking.
• Use the space above cabinets to display oversize baskets, pitchers, platters, or trays.
• Balance white cabinets with walls painted in soft tones for a look that's cozy, not chilly.
• Hang a picture rail along one wall to showcase favorite photographs. Change the display periodically.
• Store books and magazines in a wicker basket or copper washtub to enjoy with morning coffee.
• Keep the table set for drop-in company with pretty place mats and napkins tucked into attractive rings.
• Store the fixings for an impromptu coffee klatsch on the counter in a weathered tool or knife box.
• Gather a collection of easy-care cloth napkins in an ironstone bowl or garden urn for daily use.
• Set the table with pillar candles in glass hurricanes for dining ambience.

- Arrange cocktail supplies on a tray placed on a sideboard or hutch.
- Position an easy chair or two near a window for chats.
- Add a second sink or prep area so two cooks can work simultaneously.
- Make a place for school supplies so kids can do homework at the kitchen counter while you cook.
- Keep fresh flowers in a favorite vase on a countertop.
- Delight little visitors with jars filled with candy.
- Build a banquette along one wall to store entertaining supplies and serve as extra seating.
- Stack a series of racks on one wall to store wine, extra bottles of soda, and sparkling water.
- Keep an attractive liquid-hand-soap dispenser and towels near the kitchen sink for washup before meals.
- Paint a checkerboard pattern on kitchen floors for fun and to disguise worn surfaces.
- Fill glass bottles with colored water and set them in front of a window to create your own rainbows.
- Mount a fold-down table on one wall—so you can share a cup of coffee or tea with a friend in even the smallest of kitchens.

- Hang up a message board for daily reminders or to post the dinner's menu.
- Keep mugs on personalized hooks.
- Encourage family members and guests to get involved by keeping extra aprons and dish towels in sight.
- Attach baskets to the wall to hold each family member's mail.
- Fill a basket with slippers in various sizes so guests can kick off their shoes and make themselves at home.
- Welcome four-legged visitors with a ready supply of treats.
- Enliven a plain wooden table with a bright runner.

ABOVE: Chicken-wire inserts open up cabinet doors. Along with open shelves, they show off dishes to guests and add a homey touch.

LEFT: A wall organizer holds not just notes, but kitchen utensils.

Two guests that can't go away

IN REDOING AND EXPANDING THE KITCHEN in a timber-frame home in southern New Hampshire, designer Thomas R. Kelly, CKD, of Northshore Kitchens Plus in Marblehead, Massachusetts, faced a problem that couldn't go away: two structural posts smack in the center of the space. His solution needed to absorb both of those posts seamlessly into the design.

As luck would have it, one of the immovable posts stood exactly where the designer and the homeowners wanted to build a large island. That certainly posed a challenge. To unravel the conundrum, Kelly wrapped a three-level, six-sided island around the base of the post.

A copper-lined planter surrounds the post at the point where it appears to penetrate the island. The homeowners fill the planter with potting soil and grow herbs and flowers. The lowest level of the island contains an undermount vegetable sink, also made of copper. The third level is granite, at a height that's excellent both for ordinary work and for casual dining and drinks when company comes to visit.

As a person walks around this island, every little facet of the structure offers up another option. Most obvious, of course, are spaces to stand and prepare meals as well as a place to sit and enjoy them. Cushioned high-backed stools pull up to an angular extension of the countertop. In addition, the island contains open shelves for storing cookbooks and cookware, and closed cabinets provide storage for tableware and other kitchen essentials. The second post, near the back wall, received a similar treatment. The designer specified base cabinets around that post, trimming inches off cabinets in order to squeeze in as much storage space as possible.

Kelly also had to face the challenge of working in an established architectural style while tailoring the functional and spatial aspects of the house to its new owners. Adding 250 square feet to the 450-square-foot kitchen certainly gave the designer enough room to arrange cooking and dining elements without clutter, even while adhering to the wood-heavy, geometric design. The space seamlessly connects old areas to new. It's totally integrated, and thanks to the angled

ABOVE: The warming drawer sits conveniently below the cooktop.

OPPOSITE: The vaulted ceiling of the breakfast room addition makes an elegant family dining space. New tall windows look out on a woodland view.

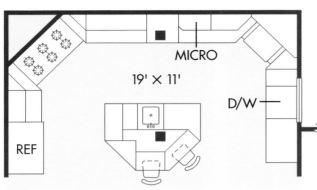

MICRO

19' × 11'

D/W

REF

ABOVE: The expanded kitchen integrates meal-prep and dining areas while incorporating two existing structural posts.

RIGHT: Two fixed posts frame an opening that separates the cooking and dining areas.

cabinets, the traffic flows easily. Anyone can move from the bar to the eating area without getting in the way of whoever is preparing a meal.

Overhead, in the addition that Kelly designed, he created an open shelf on which his clients could store and display anything that would add color and character to the kitchen. This offers an ideal opportunity for the homeowners to mark this space with their own personality, using whatever antiques or collectibles they've gathered over the years. Also worth noting is that if their taste in collectibles changes over the years, or if they sell the home, this space for personality offers quick and easy adaptability.

The granite-top island anchors two cooking zones: one includes a refrigerator and cooktop; the other, the undercounter oven and microwave.

Tying the entire space together is new oak flooring that contrasts neatly with the butternut cabinets Kelly designed. He feels that when he approaches a project such as this one, he needs to do more than design cabinets and pick out appliances and countertops. In making sure all the lines got due attention, from floor to ceiling, he helped this kitchen grow, both in size and sophistication.

ABOVE LEFT: On the island, a copper vegetable sink is tucked behind the copper-lined plant basin surrounding one of the structural posts.

ABOVE: On the beam over the peninsula is space for culinary collectibles.

LEFT: Angled in one corner are an apron-front sink and a counter designed for rolling out dough. A dishwasher is below it (behind the towel).

Where the art is

THIS RADICALLY RECONCEIVED SPACE IS ALL ABOUT materials, atmosphere, and art. Before Gioi Tran and Vernon Applegate, of Applegate Tran Interiors in San Francisco, took on the job, though, the original space was large but inefficient. It needed to be renovated extensively to meet the homeowners' needs for a contemporary yet highly functional kitchen. By opening the space to the dining room and front entry, they created a more gracious layout and brought in more natural light, plus postcard views of San Francisco Bay and the striking coastal panorama of Marin County to the north.

The homeowners grew up in Hawaii and wanted a look that was clean and minimal, with an Asian feel but also warm and inviting. They wanted place for artwork, too. After extensive planning, which involved opening the kitchen to both the dining room and the entryway of the home, the focus shifted to creating a distinctive mix of natural and man-made materials within the kitchen.

Furniture-like custom cabinets of vertical-grain eucalyptus veneer create a light, neutral backdrop that contrasts with the richer, more variegated grain of the oiled African doussie wood floor, which continues into the dining and living rooms. The doussie will darken as it ages. Absolute-black granite countertops and a golden-toned backsplash round out the palette of natural materials. The stone surfaces have a honed rather than polished finish, giving them a matte appearance, not rustic but natural. One small but emphatically earthy accent is the roughly chiseled edge of a shelf cut of the same marble and set into the backsplash.

Complementing this tactile array of wood and stone are clear and frosted glass (in cabinet doors and on the raised eating counter), stainless steel, concrete (in the structural column), and even drywall, fashioned into the sculptural counter supports of the

OPPOSITE: Ten canvases on a dark red wall form an alluring focal point for a nontraditional kitchen.

BELOW: The playful geometry of the room is clear in its mix of straight and arcing lines and forms. Pendant lights shaded with amber glass imbue the island and eating area with a soft glow.

island and faux-painted to match the concrete. Using concrete here would have been prohibitively expensive to fabricate and engineer.

Lighting is unobtrusive, consisting of recessed ceiling spots and a trio of tiny, amber glass–shaded pendant lamps over the island. To further minimize visual clutter, a television, easily viewable from seats at the island, hides in the cabinet over the wall ovens, and a built-in coffee system occupies a niche in the display cabinet next to the refrigerator. The appliance stores and grinds the coffee beans and prepares each cup of brew to order.

Despite the care taken in selecting the materials, the design of the room doesn't immediately call attention to them, a quality that helped this project earn the National Kitchen & Bath Association's top prize for design excellence. The first thing one sees upon entering is an art wall—something the homeowners considered a must—that displays a suite of 10 paintings. Painted deep red to act as a focal point, the wall is anchored by a sleek, cantilevered buffet. The arrangement creates a sense of mystery, one of the designers says, because guests hardly realize they're entering a kitchen.

In the buffet, as in a number of the other cabinets, the designers adapted Asian-style hardware by giving it unique contemporary detailing. Recessed stainless steel drawer pulls have been set as far off-center as possible on the drawer fronts without compromising the ability of the drawers to open and close smoothly. The treatment of those pulls neatly embodies the philosophy expressed in this kitchen. An architect friend of the owners suggested they add a second column for symmetry, but they didn't take the suggestion, even though architects know a thing or two about design. The thing is, this design isn't really about symmetry.

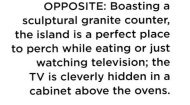

OPPOSITE: Boasting a sculptural granite counter, the island is a perfect place to perch while eating or just watching television; the TV is cleverly hidden in a cabinet above the ovens.

BELOW: A backsplash of golden marble flanks absolute-black granite countertops and custom cabinets finished in vertical-grain eucalyptus.

BELOW RIGHT: The designers revitalized this kitchen by opening it up to the dining room and front entry.

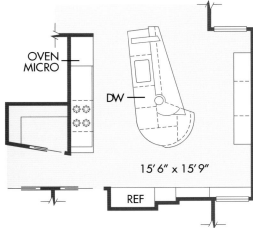

OVEN
MICRO

DW

15' 6" x 15' 9"

REF

WHICH IS A MORE IMPORTANT FACTOR IN CHOOSING MATERIALS, COLOR OR TEXTURE?

Color and texture are intimately related because color depends on the reflectivity of light. Texture affects that reflectivity, so it also affects color; the same color will look different on surfaces of different texture.

If you paint a flat expanse of drywall a particular color and skim-coat another surface with integrally colored plaster tinted the identical hue, they won't look the same. In part this is because the pigment isn't dispersed as evenly through the plaster as it is through the paint, and in part, it's because the color will have greater depth and subtlety on the rougher plaster surface thanks to the play of light and shadow. Similarly, the same color paint applied to smooth-troweled plaster and to textured plaster will appear different.

When it comes to kitchens in particular, there's a heightened awareness today that germs can lurk in textured surfaces, and the smoothest textures are the easiest to keep clean. But a kitchen done in all stainless steel can be cold and clinical. What's most practical isn't always the most aesthetically pleasing solution.

43 WAYS TO ADD STORAGE SPACE

A VERITABLE WAREHOUSE of space sits unused in almost every kitchen. Extra storage awaits in unexpected sources. Take advantage of wasted space under cabinets, in drawers, behind toekicks or on walls, and add drawer inserts, lazy Susans, and slide-out shelves. Read on for more storage-stretching tips.

ABOVE: Lids for pots and pans can be elusive at exactly the wrong time. Stop searching and store them on a roll-out rack.

RIGHT: Tame the chaos of loose utensils by installing a stainless steel hanging rod above the counter.

- Hang utensils from a rod attached to a wall area near the stove.
- Suspend pots from a ceiling rack or hang them from grids.
- Install deep rolling drawers for pots. Extra depth and ease of access translate into more storage.
- Fill an oversize cup and saucer with teaspoons to make room in drawers for other cutlery.
- Store baking essentials—cupcake tins, candy molds, cake pans—on shallow, rolling metal shelves installed under counters.
- Fit a drawer with a chopping block and inserts for knives.

- Attach a magnetic strip near your prep area to corral frequently used knives and other utensils.
- Organize spices with horizontal drawer inserts or in a narrow, vertical pullout cabinet near the cooktop.
- Surround a doorway with Shaker-style boxes to hold wine bottles, mugs, or decorative items.
- Hang a collection of coffee cups on wall-mounted racks.
- Install grids under the tops of cabinets to hold stemware.
- Hide oversize appliances in "garages" under a cabinet.
- Tuck a step stool or extra supplies in drawers designed to fill the toekick area under cabinets.
- Turn the space between wall studs into a shallow cabinet for mops, an ironing board, or spice shelves.
- Add sleek storage with metal baker's racks. Oversize bowls fit well on the deep shelves. Be sure to attach locking casters so the units can be moved as needed.
- Compartmentalize cutlery using specially designed trays. In deeper drawers, stack units for greater storage; the top unit slides back to reveal the contents of the lower one.
- Display favorite collectibles such as egg cups or salt and pepper shakers on custom-designed shelves positioned under standard cabinets.
- Hang holders for rolls of foil or plastic on an interior cabinet door.
- Install pot-lid racks on sliding tracks in a base cabinet.

- Stack cans and jars in cabinets to take advantage of height.
- Mount a coffeemaker under a cabinet near cups and coffee canisters.
- Use lazy Susans to access items stored in corner units.
- Turn the inside of a door into a message center by lining it with corkboard.
- Replace a standard base cabinet with a divided unit for trash and recyclables.
- Keep pet food handy in a pullout bin.
- Hang a dish-drying rack that folds up when not in use.
- Fold and store kitchen towels on an expandable wooden towel rack.
- Attach a brass rail around the perimeter of a freestanding island to hold pots, pans, and utensils.
- Place a stainless steel container in an out-of-the-way corner to hold mixers, large bowls, and stockpots.
- Gain extra shelf space in a cupboard by transferring stemware to a wooden or wire undercabinet holder.
- Hang brooms and dustpans in plain sight from an old-fashioned standing coat rack. Add colorful aprons and dish towels to the mix.
- Store baking equipment on a rolling cart; stow it in a closet when not in use, or, if floor space permits, let it double as a movable kitchen island.
- Install pull-down shelf units in wall cabinets. They make otherwise-unreachable top shelves accessible for everyday use.
- Avoid teetering towers of cups and mugs by hanging them separately inside a cabinet on hooks screwed into the bottom of the shelf above.
- Outfit cabinet bases with shallow drawers to hold large platters and cookie sheets.
- Mount a series of rustic sap buckets in a column on the wall to hold mixing spoons, rolling pins and whisks.
- Install a wall grid or Peg-Board to hold pot lids, utensils, paper goods, and holders for other kitchen necessities.

This pull-down rack brings the highest shelves, normally the province of little-used items, within easy reach, resulting in more room for everyday items.

- Display pot holders and dish towels on a section of wood trellis that has been securely attached to the wall.
- Fill sections of muffin tins with kitchen odds and ends.
- Turn the space behind the false panels in front of your kitchen sink into a storage area—an easy DIY project with a tilt-out drawer front kit from your local hardware store.
- Free up counter or drawer space by mounting an electric can opener under a cabinet or a knife holder inside a door.
- To keep track of the bottoms of springform pans, buy two magnets for each bottom. Glue one to the inside of a cabinet door, apply the pan bottom, then stick on the other magnet.
- In small kitchens, store little-used items in other areas like the dining room, laundry room, or basement.

Retire-mint

HERE'S A MINTY-FRESH IDEA for those nearing their leisure years: A retirement home near the University of California-Davis allows its occupants full access to the campus and, as shown here, full remodeling rights. This generic 900-square-foot apartment got the full treatment from Cheng Design in Berkeley, California. Designers Fu-Tung Cheng and Cathleen Quandt used a mix of natural materials and shifting planes to transform the kitchen into a contemporary space that's still the functional heart of the loft home and accessible to residents of all ages.

The two designers strove for a dramatic yet calm motif, according to Cheng, who regards his work passionately enough to use words like "equanimity." Dropped-ceiling panels at 7- and 8-foot heights overlap as they step from the living area into the dining and kitchen areas. Soft, glowing light issues from above the panels to cast the apartment in warmth. Rich cherry cabinets give depth of color, and a cherry shelf extends at waist height perpendicular to the serving counter that bridges the kitchen and the dining room. Under this shelf is a maple dining table that pulls out to seat extra guests.

A cast-concrete sculpture—easily the most striking visual element—serves as the hub of the kitchen, the entry to the apartment, the dining area, and the library hallway. The piece incorporates a kitchen counter that works as a bar or buffet when the couple hosts friends. The designers used the simple geometry to keep the spaces open and flowing while still separating them. Another concrete counter, slightly lower and fronting the dining area, forms a T with the larger piece. The counters feature a touch Cheng Design is known for: evocative objects embedded in the mix, such as a shard of pottery and ancient ammonite shells.

The kitchen is a testament to natural materials that look best undisguised, like wood (of course) and limestone tiles on the wall. The tiles, in gently varied shades of taupe, share the wall with accent strips of slate tile, creating a textural variation that appears as though the squares were blocks jutting out to various depths—though in

PRECEDING PAGES: What looks like a bent slab of concrete instantly grabs attention and lends emphatic stylistic character to a kitchen that measures only 7x11 feet.

ABOVE: A stainless steel sink sits behind the counter and the concrete sculpture that hides cleanup and dishes from view.

OPPOSITE ABOVE: Shelves in place of wall cabinets keep the space visually open; limestone wall tiles provide color contrast.

OPPOSITE BELOW: One of Cheng Design's most sought-after products is this sleek range hood. Cherry cabinets provide more color interest.

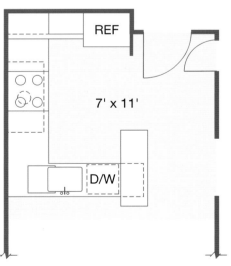

REF

7' x 11'

D/W

reality the wall is flat. Contrasting this rugged character is sleek stainless steel in the counters, sink, backsplash, refrigerator, range hood, and open shelves. The cherry of the cabinets, maple of the table, and bamboo flooring all came from sustainable forests, for the environmentally aware.

Cabinets weren't a priority. For one thing, having a lot of food on hand is redundant in a retirement community with a shared dining hall, and for another, the cabinets would overwhelm. Besides, these designers tend to avoid upper wall cabinets. So the right designers found the right project.

CONTEMPORARY KITCHEN SECRETS

MATERIAL INTEREST Limestone tiles in varied buff tones, punctuated by decorative lines of slate and thin steel shelving, give a multiplanar appearance to the back wall.

RETRACTABLE TABLE The homeowners can pull the dining table out from under a cherry shelf when guests stop by.

CONCEALED STORAGE An appliance garage with cherry tambour door houses the microwave and toaster oven; outlets are inside.

SMALLER-SCALE APPLIANCES For a space geared to minimal, not elaborate, cooking, a 27-inch refrigerator has the right proportions.

LOW-MAINTENANCE FINISHES Easy-to-clean stainless steel counters and backsplash nicely offset the rougher stone and concrete textures.

HALF-WALLS A cast-concrete partition functions as a counter and as the main element that visually divides the kitchen area from the rest of the home.

NO CUPBOARDS Using only drawers in place of base cabinets makes it easy for the homeowners to find what they need without stooping.

See-worthy

A CABINET DEDICATED TO CRAB POTS and a drawer stacked with bibs and claw crackers are a tip-off that this kitchen is in a home near Maryland's Chesapeake Bay. When attorney Christopher Suss built a 4,000-square-foot house directly on the shore, he was determined that the kitchen feel as if it were floating on the water—one reason that he insisted the room be on the second floor. As a place where he and his girlfriend would dine, the kitchen had to foster the sense of expansiveness boaters experience on the water.

Christopher hired designer Jennifer Gilmer, CKD—his sister, it just so happens—to fashion a room where two people could enjoy eating together and feel an intimate connection with the sea. She chose highly reflective elements that evoke shimmering water. She also purposely used curvy shapes to create a fluid feel in the space. As much as practical, the kitchen avoids hard, 90-degree angles (from a countertop standpoint, at least).

To help create the effect of waves, Gilmer used inch-square blue-glass tiles for the backsplash, which rises to the ceiling on a sinuous wall, intended to evoke the prow of a boat. The stainless steel range hood resides on this wall. Blue granite countertops on the island and elsewhere, and a cobalt-blue glass eating shelf on the island add to the effect, as do the complementary hanging lamps of—guess what color? That's right: blue. Christopher had lobbied to use teak, a common material used in boats, for the cabinets. Alas, teak is an oily wood, and it can be difficult to work. In particular, teak is hard to cut accurately, which makes it especially dicey to use in kitchens, where the motto "Measure twice; cut once" is drilled into every contractor's brain to reinforce the importance of accuracy.

The appropriate and less costly alternative Gilmer chose was bubinga, a deep-red African wood with a vibrant grain, for two conspicuous areas of the room: as a custom panel on the refrigerator and on a similarly scaled cabinet on the opposite side of the kitchen.

Elsewhere in the kitchen, Gilmer used maple, notably on the eating island. The chosen maple is not typical, however. It is a quartersawn maple, meaning the grain comes out on the horizontal. The lines in the wood make the eyes move horizontally through the room.

Nightly, Christopher and his girlfriend drop anchor at the island for dinner. Two upholstered stools fit comfortably in a 6-foot recess, which is

ABOVE: Glassware and wines sit in side-by-side units on one of the island's outer faces. This setup is perfect for the party host; serving thirsty guests is easy, and the location diverts them away from the main work area.

OPPOSITE: The materials and forms used in the kitchen create a lively composition—especially important in an open-plan space.

divided by a turned-maple post. The 3/4-inch-thick glass shelf is elevated 6 inches above the countertop and is supported by polished chrome pillars. "I like contemporary styles, especially in the kitchen," Christopher says.

Judging from what Gilmer says, plenty of homeowners want to knock down the wall that separates the formal dining area from the kitchen. The tendency to entertain formally is decidedly on the wane, and more and more remodeling customers want a couple of stools and a place in the kitchen to eat.

To make the eating-in experience especially efficient, Gilmer ensured the island gave access to everything needed during the course of a meal. A wine refrigerator is next to a glass-front cabinet with wineglasses; a similar cabinet holds dishes.

For many homeowners, especially those who entertain often, a kitchen needs to be the focus of the home without being showy. To achieve this balance, Gilmer keeps wall cabinets to a minimum, with the majority of storage relegated to a walk-in pantry, as she did with Christopher's kitchen. Open display shelves above the prep sink and on either side of the cooktop come off more as built-in pieces than as cabinets. The stools, too, are as much plush din-

ABOVE: A handsome column of stainless steel appliances—microwave, built-in coffeemaker, and wall oven—is situated at one end of the kitchen.

RIGHT: Essentially a pair of L-shaped counters that open onto one another, the kitchen is cleverly laid out in a design that balances the public and private aspects of the room.

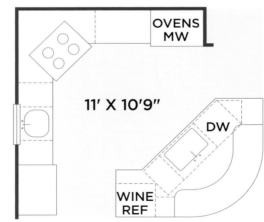

ing chairs as they are pragmatically placed perches.

That unassuming practicality is a good thing, given the frequency with which those chairs are used. "My girlfriend especially likes to eat at the island," Christopher says. "She says it's as comfortable as being at a table, but she doesn't feel that we're at a counter. Sometimes we just sit there enjoying a nice glass of wine while steaks cook on the grill or crab pots boil away on the stove."

TABLE SERVICE

When planning a kitchen island meant for serious dining, consider the following:

• Although your dining companion is usually the best focal point, all diners like to have views from the table. Locate the eating area to capture light and views.

• Design the eating surface so that most utensils, dishware, and other necessities are close at hand.

• Allow room to place hot and cold dishes within reach.

• Side-by-side seating is fine, but it can make conversation difficult. A curved eating surface allows people to sit next to each other and chat comfortably.

• Make the eating area versatile: as a dining surface, a place for the chef's adoring spectators, a location for hard-studying children, or a buffet.

ABOVE: The ovens (when not in use) can be concealed by a door made of bubinga wood, which matches the custom paneling on the refrigerator that stands directly across the room.

RIGHT: The marine-blue mosaic tiles on the backsplash are a colorful nod to the kitchen's seaside locale. The iridescent quality mimics sunlight playing on the waters of the bay outside. The effect continues with the blue granite of the countertops.

ABOVE: The bi-level island defines the outer edge of the kitchen without closing it off from either exterior views or indoor spaces.

RIGHT: An instant hot-water dispenser is one of those essential conveniences in a busy household.

Sharp dressed

THIS HOMEOWNER HAD A VISION. Her vision was a dramatically contemporary home and an urban kitchen. One of the keystones of her kitchen was the color: strictly neutral. That's why this kitchen is exclusively black, white, gray, and silver.

So interior designer John Kazmir, of St. Catherines, Ontario, applied his craft to this 3,800-square-foot home on the shore of Lake Ontario. With his work and the homeowner's vision, the home makes a consistent statement throughout. It all starts with a modern glass-and-stucco exterior, continuing on to an open-riser stairway and polished-granite flooring. Nowhere, however, is the style of the house more fully expressed than in the kitchen.

"I appreciate other looks I see in magazines, but my eye always goes to contemporary designs," says the homeowner, who gathered clippings of the kind of clean-lined look she wanted before she sat down to discuss her ideas with Kazmir.

Gray-stained wood was the first cabinet suggestion, but finding a stain that didn't take on a taupe cast was impossible. The eventual solution was a high-gloss gray lacquer with tiny metallic flakes. Complementing the lacquer are countertops of darker gray-flannel granite, with minute silvery flecks and not much pattern, and a floor of a different granite, a mixture of white and gray. The flooring was ordered in 18-inch squares that were ½ inch thick. (Floor tiles larger than 12 inches should be thicker than the standard ⅜ inch to prevent cracking.) They are laid in a tight, invisible-seam application that looks like a solid stone slab. The subtle sparkle of the lacquer and stone is particularly delightful at night, when the light of the recessed ceiling cans and above-cabinet units hits them.

Glass and brushed stainless steel further develop the modern aesthetic of the kitchen. Some of the smaller wall cabinets have glass doors. A pantry with a sandblasted-glass front relieves the expanse of lacquered cabinets that surrounds the oven, panes the refrigerator, and conceals the espresso maker and microwave. The pantry glass is slightly translucent but won't let a person read cereal box labels

PRECEDING PAGES: The open floor plan encourages long views through the house; the dining area overlooks the family room, which sits a few steps down from the kitchen level.

ABOVE: Diners seated at the breakfast bar can enjoy how wide-open the room is. Large windows, high ceilings, and clean-lined cabinets contribute to the effect—one that enhances the atmosphere of a contemporary space.

through it. Responding to the homeowner's concern that a frosted surface would be a haven for fingerprints, the cabinet fabricator made each door from a stack of two thin sheets of glass, with sandblasted sides facing each other, so the outer surface is easy to clean inside and out. The cantilevered breakfast bar is also made of sandblasted glass, which, like the sculptural range hood and the two wall cabinets flanking the cooktop, has curves that soften the preponderance of straight lines in the kitchen. Aluminum-framed, commercial-grade windows run up to the ceiling, providing generous expanses of glass, and over the cooktop is an east-facing wall of rectangular glass block that creates a gap of light between the radius-front cabinets (at least during the day).

The heavy-duty aesthetic refinement of the kitchen in no way indicates that it is more a showcase than a functional family cooking and gathering space. Designer Irene Wiens, CKD, worked hard to ensure that above all, this kitchen was a functional space as she consulted with Kazmir and his client on the layout of the room.

"I've always wanted a contemporary home," says the woman, who shares the space with her husband and two kids, "but we're a family; we wanted to make the room as child-friendly as possible." She adds, "Most of our guests are couples with kids, too." Groups gather at the large eating-area table, beyond which are the sunken family room and views that extend all the way to the opposite shore of the lake. Grown-up guests chat with the cook from the breakfast-bar side of the island. Practicality reigns throughout. Base cabinets rise to 38 inches, a full 2 inches higher than standard, to accommodate the tall couple; materials and surfaces are not just attractive but easy to maintain. The owner points out that the secondary sink located on the center island is functional on a full-scale level. "It's not just a little bar sink," she says. "At 15 inches in diameter, it's really useful for things like draining large pots."

Beauty and practicality: These qualities are inseparable in this kitchen. Kazmir, the interior designer, feels it's a piece of art. The woman tempers that statement a little, saying, "We work in this kitchen all the time." But when she says, "I love to stand and work at the island, with a view of Toronto across the water," it's clear that work and pleasure merge into one experience in this striking room.

ABOVE: Floating the cooktop cabinets against a floor-to-ceiling expanse of glass block is a dramatic—and definitely contemporary—way of bringing light and definition to the room. Laid on end, the glass blocks emphasize the height of the space.

ABOVE: Along the inside wall of the room, a serving counter relieves the boxy volumes of the refrigerator and the full-height pantry.

OPPOSITE: Sandblasted glass doors conceal tall pantry cabinets. Adding this finish to the mix of materials prevents the gray lacquer from overwhelming the kitchen.

COOL APPLIANCES

Cutting-edge appliances are a must for city style. Sleek designs complete the look of a contemporary kitchen, and technologically advanced features offer quick, easy alternatives for people with busy lifestyles. For example, the newest ranges and ovens cut cooking time substantially, and are much easier to clean than older models.

TOP: This 36-inch cooktop features five sealed gas burners, continuous platform grates, and a spill basin for easy cleanup.

ABOVE: For old-fashioned cooking and modern convenience, a dual-fuel, 30-inch built-in traditional range features convection baking, a cooktop with an extra-low simmer setting on two of its four sealed burners, an oven vent, and a self-cleaning system.

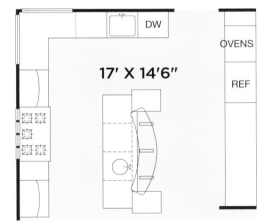

DW

OVENS

17' X 14'6"

REF

ABOVE: Built-in appliances around the perimeter of the room keep the floor plan of the kitchen organized and functional.

ABOVE: Raising the base cabinets up on slender steel legs keeps them from appearing bottom-heavy and monolithic—important in a cool-colored kitchen like this one. In addition, it makes cleaning easier.

Cooktops

IN KITCHENS WHERE ONE COOK SAUTÉS while another bakes, the cooktop and oven must go their separate ways. Another part of this book will cover ovens, but here are the major factors to consider when choosing a cooktop.

GAS OR ELECTRIC?

Deciding on a gas or electric cooktop is the first step. Professional chefs prefer gas because the heat level adjusts quickly. Those who have always cooked electric shouldn't rule out gas, though. Kitchen designers say switching from electric to gas can be as simple as contacting the utility company and having a gas line installed. If that's not possible, a propane tank can accomplish the same results.

In addition to quick adjustments, the advantages of gas cooktops include models with special high- and low-heat burners that can sear (up to 16,000 Btu, great for steaks) or simmer (600 Btu, for delicate sauces). Sealed burners, a common feature in gas cooktops, prevent spills from creating messes beneath the surface of the appliance. Some gas models have continuous grates, which allow you to slide heavy pots and pans across the cooking surface without lifting, and burners that reignite automatically if blown out.

Although most serious cooks gravitate toward gas, electric cooktops still get the job done just fine. Sure, the glowing coils are still around, but electric cooktops have gone so far beyond that.

Ceramic-glass cooktops are made of a durable material that conducts heat well and cleans up easily because it's perfectly flat. These models come with one of two burner types: radiant or halogen. Radiant burners, more common and less expensive, have concealed circular ribbon elements that glow when hot. Halogen burners blast heat from a powerful lightbulb that warms quickly and reacts rapidly to temperature adjustments. For this reason, halogen burners are the most gas-like of all the electric cooktops in terms of responsiveness. Push-button controls on more advanced radiant and halogen models provide more accurate temperature regulation.

Dual heating elements (single burners that combine a 6- and a 9-inch, or a 9- and a 12-inch element, in one location) are popping up on some radiant and halogen designs. These dual elements are more flexible because they allow the cook to match the burner size to the pot size for optimum heat distribution.

This gas cooktop is designed for easy cleanup, with sealed burners and porcelain-coated cast-iron grates.

The continuous grate on this cooktop lets the cook move pots without lifting. The unit also has a fifth burner in the middle.

STANDARD SIZES

Gas and electric cooktops come in several standard widths: 15, 30, 36, 45 and 48 inches. The most popular configurations are 30 and 36 inches, with four or five burners each. The 15-inch units are single- or dual-burner models, used alone or in combination with grills, fryers, or other similar-size modules. The 45- and 48-inch behemoths are the professional-style models, with a minimum of four burners and options for adding accessories like grills and griddles.

The National Kitchen & Bath Association advises allowing plenty of elbow room on both sides of the cooktop, for safety, convenience, and pot handles. In an open-ended countertop run, a minimum of 12 inches of countertop must be on one side of the cooktop, with 15 inches on the other side. In a closed run (between walls, say), have at least 3 inches between the cooktop and a flame-retardant wall, and at least 15 inches on the opposite side. Also, installing a heat-resistant countertop surface adjacent to the cooktop will provide a convenient landing place for hot pans.

GOOD These cooktops are simple, no-frills, black or white 30-inch units with four burners and standard knob-style controls. On electric models, coil elements and chrome drip bowls are the norm. With gas, it's stamped-metal grates and sealed burners. Hint: If the cooktop is in a store that also sells DVD players and car stereos, it may just be a "good" cooktop.

BETTER Take a step up in style and performance. On electric models, look for smooth ceramic-glass tops with radiant ribbon elements and control knobs that lift off for easy cleaning.
Dual-watt elements make an appearance at the upper ends of this category. If gas is more your style, expect to find cast-iron grates and higher Btu outputs. Whether you want gas or electric, look for larger models (36 inches) with five burners and the option of built-in downdraft venting. Color choices for both include black, white, and off-white.

BEST Extra burners, improved performance, and sleek stainless steel finishes are three reasons to consider these models. Look for increased flame control on gas models, with high-heat (12,000 Btu) and simmer (850 Btu) burners common. Gas burners in this category should also be equipped with devices that automatically reignite the flame if it blows out. With electric, expect to find a wide variety of element sizes and controls that constantly monitor and adjust heat output for precise and consistent temperature control.

ULTRA These professional-style designs offer four to six burners and have all the modern amenities. With gas, expect to find high-performance burners with precision controls that range from a 12,000-Btu searing blue flame to a delicate 600-Btu flicker. Electric designs use halogen-heating technology to reach full power in seconds. Bridge elements, which allow two burners to function as one, are also common. Options include grills, griddles, and wok modules.

Pro-Style Ranges

A COMMERCIAL-STYLE RANGE provides more than vicarious wish fulfillment for avid cooks whose friends keep telling them, "You should open a restaurant!" At the same time, they're also more than aggressive design statements for the deep-pocketed. Truth is, they're both of these and more.

One key to understanding commercial-style appliances is to heed the word style. Actual restaurant ranges are hotter and less insulated than those in homes. So although it's possible to put a real commercial range in a residential kitchen, the installation must include powerful ventilation and extensive insulation between the range and pretty much everything else to prevent the kitchen from catching fire every time the range is turned on. (They're that powerful.) Be aware that it's illegal in many states to use a true commercial range in a residence.

Commercial-style ranges, on the other hand, combine the safety benefits of household gas ranges (insulation, burners with automatic ignition) with the professional features (high-heat burners, oversize ovens) that give commercial ranges such sizzle, both literally and figuratively.

IMPROVED PERFORMANCE

One reason restaurant chefs prize their commercial ranges is the high-heat cooktops. Burners can crank out 18,000 to 20,000 Btu, which can cut in half the time it takes to sear a steak. Commercial-style residential ranges have slightly less oomph—15,000 to 16,000 Btu is normal. That still adds up to a quick dinner, but flames won't be shooting 6 inches above the grate. (A standard gas range maxes out at roughly 9,000 Btu.)

This high-power attitude continues below the cooktop. There, larger-than-normal convection ovens (typically 4.8 cubic feet rather than the standard 4.0) equipped with restaurant-style broilers can cut baking and broiling times in half. Some ovens have infrared broilers that can reach 1,500° F in seconds, like

GOOD Expect to find a basic 30-inch all-gas range with four 15,000-Btu burners and a single 4.8-cubic-foot oven with at least two racks. Burner grates should be made of heavy-duty, porcelainized cast iron and should be removable for easy cleaning.

BETTER All-gas models are still the standard; however, you can find a few dual-fuel ranges that combine 15,000-Btu gas cooktops with self-cleaning electric ovens. Look for 36-inch models that offer an expanded cooking surface—typically six burners, or four burners with either a grill or griddle.

BEST The major difference between these and "better" models is cooking capacity. Look for 48- and 60-inch offerings that accommodate two electric or gas ovens and a minimum of six gas burners and grill, griddle, or wok attachments. As on all pro-style models, the gas burners on these models go from a 15,000-Btu high to a 500-Btu low in seconds.

the salamander that restaurants use to put that just-so crispy char on steaks while keeping the insides extra juicy. These high-end home ranges also provide more control over the cooking process. One manufacturer's simmer-plate attachment holds heat at a steady 135° F—ideal for soups and sauces. Another's burners maintain such an even, low temperature that they can melt chocolate without a double boiler.

SIZED TO FIT

Although these monster models approximate the real thing, they don't necessarily require a restaurant-size kitchen. The smallest models will fit a meager 24-inch gap. The standard 30-inch range is also available, as are 36- and 48-inch models. For those with 5 feet of continuous, otherwise-unused kitchen space, more than one company makes 60-inch ranges, with two full-size ovens and six or eight burners and a bevy of options. Now, that's cooking with gas.

Other than price, the primary caveat when considering commercial-style cooking equipment is the need for adequate ventilation in the form of a mighty vent hood to remove steam and grease from the air. Weak ventilation would allow grease particles to collect in the hood. Couple that with the intense heat of the commercial-style range (more heat than a typical furnace), and the result is an increased fire risk.

An exhaust system for an old-fashioned range would move about 160 cubic feet of air in a minute, otherwise listed as 160 cfm. This won't cut it for a commercial-style range. More cooking power means more heat, steam, and grease. Determining proper ventilation requirement means consulting the range manufacturer's specifications. The wise homeowner will also consult a professional on this matter.

Speaking of fire, the wall behind the range should be fireproof. Tile and brick are OK, because both materials are fire retardant. Otherwise, the wall should take a back guard, a piece of stainless steel that rises from the cooktop to the hood.

USER-FRIENDLY

True commercial ranges are a pain to clean. Fortunately, this is just one more disadvantage engineered out in the transition from restaurant to residence. Commercial-style ranges are as easy to care for as typical household stoves. Current models come with sealed burners and self-cleaning ovens—even on gas models.

Finish is another factor. The most common choice is stainless steel, of course. Despite being handsome and, well, stainless, it's not as fuss-free as one might expect. Apparently, stainless steel never met a fingerprint it didn't like. Thankfully, special cleaners are readily available to keep every stainless steel surface as fresh as the day it was made. One company offers its ranges in colors, including black, blue, green, and burgundy. These generally require less pampering.

Ventilation Systems

A POT OF SOUP SIMMERING ON THE STOVE, vegetables stir-frying in a wok, and a steak sizzling on an indoor grill…it all sounds tasty, but they all send off a lot of residue that doesn't belong in the air. The more adventurous the cooking in a kitchen, particularly on the cooktop, the more ventilation it needs.

Grease, smoke, and cooking odors can cling to walls, ceilings, and draperies, and the combination of intense heat and water will produce condensation that can damage walls and cause paint and wallpaper to peel. Gas cooktops add nitrogen dioxide, carbon dioxide, and carbon monoxide—three toxic, unwelcome gases. Proper ventilation, however, can make all of these problems disappear, leaving a cleaner kitchen and a safer, fresher home.

CLEARING THE AIR

Practically speaking, kitchen ventilation falls into two categories: updraft and downdraft. Updraft systems install directly over the cooking surface, be it on an island or along the wall. In either case, the ventilation system, housed in a vent hood, gathers contaminated vapors that rise naturally during the cooking process and traffics them to the outside using a blower that pushes them through a series of ducts. Because hot air rises naturally, updraft has physics in its favor.

Downdraft designs, integrated into the surface of some ranges and cooktops, function by pulling dirty air across the cooking plane and down through an exhaust duct that leads outside the home. Downdraft is popular on islands, peninsulas, and other places where a clean line of sight overhead has some benefit. Most downdraft systems are retractable; pushing a button brings the unit up for cooking and sends it back flush with the cooktop afterward. The prime drawback for this option—and it's significant—is that because downdraft units typically rise less than 10 inches above a cooking surface, they work best with low pans, and pollutants from tall pots can elude the pull of the fan. In households where all the pots are 10 inches or shorter, downdraft can work fine.

If the ducts from the hood or downdraft unit don't lead outside the house, then the kitchen doesn't really have any ventilation at all. Those over-the-range microwaves with the built-in fans tend to fall in this category. Such contraptions are more aptly labeled filtration units and have a limited ability to reduce grease, smoke, heat, and odors. Homeowners with gas appliances should particularly strive to avoid these non-vented fans, as they can't remove combustible gases

from the air, and they require regular cleaning or replacement even to serve their nominal filtration function.

POWERFUL PERFORMANCE

The performance of kitchen ventilation equipment is rated according to the volume of air a system can move in one minute. This measure, called cubic feet per minute, or cfm, varies from 100 to 1,500. The higher the number, the more efficiently the unit will evacuate contaminants from a kitchen—and the more noise it's likely to make.

Kitchen-industry standards state the minimum rating for a system installed over a standard gas or electric range or cooktop should be at least 150 cfm. With professional-style gas appliances, the minimum jumps to 600 cfm, although the wise homeowner will check the range or cooktop manufacturer's specifications before installing any ventilation system. If the Btus are particularly lofty, the 600-cfm minimum becomes insufficient.

To help simplify the purchasing process, major manufacturers have joined the Home Ventilating Institute (HVI). This nonprofit group tests products independently and certifies cfm performance ratings, helping to reduce some consumer guesswork. (Its Website, *www.hvi.org*, has more information.)

THE PERFECT FIT

For peak performance, all updraft and downdraft designs should be the same width as the cooking surface. In other words, a 30-inch range needs a hood or a downdraft vent that's at least 30 inches wide. Going a little overboard is fine, too; some designers recommend an extra 6 inches of width, 3 on each side. The hood should also be deep enough (from the wall out, for example) to reach the middle of the front burners. The distance between the cooking surface and the hood should be 18 to 24 inches, hood manufacturers say.

A hood over an island cooktop needs a more powerful motor than its wall-mounted counterpart for the same size of cooktop, because crosscurrents of air move heat and pollutants in multiple directions. A good rule of thumb is to install the hood 24 to 30 inches above the cooktop and to have all four sides

GOOD These budget-minded updraft units are perfect for basic cooktops and ranges. Minimal cfm outputs (150 is normal) make these models unfit for professional-style appliances. Expect a limited range of styles (white, black, biscuit are common color offerings) and sizes. If noise is a concern, keep in mind that these are not among the quietest units. Only the most basic downdraft units appear in this category.

BETTER A more varied selection of both updraft and downdraft designs is a reason to step up to this category. Improved feature and cfm output (500 is normal) are two more. Expect to find built-in warming lamps, remote-control, improved speed-control options for the fan and stainless steel finishes. Look for power packs that can be used to create custom designs at the upper end of this category.

BEST If design is the major concern, go straight to this category. These units quietly assert power without taking up too much space. Blowers with increased cfm capabilities are common (600 cfm is typically the minimum). Extras like heat sensor switches and the delayed–shutoff option make them more user-friendly.

of the hood extend 6 inches past the edges of the cooktop.

FINE FEATURES

Technology waits for no one, and in ventilation, advances have made cooking simpler and safer. For example, some hoods offer built-in heat sensors that switch the blower to high when the heat coming off the cooking surface reaches an unacceptable level. Delayed turnoff keeps the blower running for up to 20 minutes after the cooktop or range has been shut down, then the system turns itself off—great for the absentminded chef. Other near-essentials are lights and multiple fan speeds. Dishwasher-safe filters are a definite plus. The noise the hood makes, which everyone is sure to notice, is measured in sones. HVI also measures this and puts its ratings on its certification labels. A handy guide is that one sone is the rough equivalent of a quiet refrigerator's hum. Quiet fans measure about two sones or less.

DESIGN DETAILS

Stainless steel remains a popular hood finish, but decorative, custom-made hood surrounds have become more popular. Common options include wood, stucco, and even tile. These custom assemblies disguise what's known as a power pack—the guts of the ventilation system, without any cosmetics. Another way to shed some stainless steel from a vent hood is with glass. Hoods with glass canopies look sleek and sexy without the boxy enclosure, but they require constant cleaning to maintain that allure.

Adequate ventilation is a good investment, and not just because it keeps the kitchen from burning down. It also controls humidity in the kitchen, which in turn can keep mold and mildew at bay. On top of all that, ventilation lasts. A well-built system can survive for decades.

Wall Ovens

FROM THOSE WHOSE CULINARY GOALS are to make their own puff-pastry dough to those who merely seek the perfect frozen pizza, an oven exists to fit everyone's cooking prowess. In fact, in any given home, the main cook's preferences will determine the right oven for a kitchen remodel. The following information is an excellent warm-up for oven shopping.

HEAT SOURCES

Many of the same chefs who favor gas cooktops would much rather have an electric oven. That's because electric ovens use coils to generate heat and maintain a more consistent temperature. The bottom line is, they just cook better, and once upon a time, electric ovens were the only means of getting convection, which creates even heat throughout the oven cavity. Now, gas ovens cook just fine, just as electric cooktops do, and as implied above, technology now allows convection in gas ovens. So for the non-cooking geeks out there, the choice really comes down to personal preference.

BIGGER IS BETTER

Kitchen dimensions, family size, and cooking ambitions all factor in when you're determining the appropriate oven size. The smart shopper is the one who notes the dimensions of the current oven and consults with a designer to determine how much space is available for a new one. Standard wall ovens come 24, 27, and 30 inches wide. Some high-end manufacturers, however, have created 36-inch models that can accommodate an entire 20-pound turkey and several side dishes simultaneously. This granddaddy could be especially useful in homes where large families live or gather regularly.

DOUBLE OR SINGLE

Another strategy for large families is to get more than one oven. A double oven—one unit consisting of two ovens, or two separate ovens, one stacked atop the other—offers the option of slow-cooking a pork roast at 250°F all day in one oven and baking cookies at 375°F in the other. Stacking two single ovens in a double-oven cutout can be an energy saver. With a 24-inch oven and a 30-inch oven, a cook can choose the smaller unit for lighter duty, thereby requiring less heat.

INSTALLATION ISSUES

What kind of electrical hookup an oven needs depends largely on whether it's a single or double design. Most single wall ovens take 30-amp connections, and most doubles use 40 amps. Some high-style European designs can operate on 20-amp connections, but those are the exceptions. All ovens require a dedicated 220-volt circuit. A gas oven will also require a dedicated fuel line.

HOT AIR

Convection is not a new technology, but it has gradually seeped into the mainstream. Standard ovens have a gas or electric element that produces heat, which radiates naturally in a closed cavity. Convection ovens add a current of warm air to circulate the heat evenly. When used right, the end result is juicier roasts and consistent baked goods.

Marketing groups and manufacturers insist families keep getting busier and busier, and convection can cut baking and roasting times by as much as 30 percent. This advantage, however, is most profound for things like turkeys, which are not normal workweek fare. Then again, holiday cooking can be even more insane than normal work; so maybe those marketing groups are on to something.

Taste is another factor that has pushed convection technology to the forefront. Roasts come out browned and juicy and worthy of huzzahs.

GOOD Expect to find simple single ovens in standard 24-, 27-, and 30-inch configurations. Oven racks should be easily adjustable, and controls should be electronic. Features will be limited, but you should be able to find a self-cleaning model at the upper end of this category. Finish choices are limited to black, white, and bisque.

BETTER If you're looking for an oven that offers flexibility, this is a good place to begin. Expect to find racking systems that can easily be adjusted to fit your needs. Larger oven cavities and double designs allow you to cook more foods at once, while special sensors ensure more accurate and uniform baking temperatures. Convection cooking and stainless steel designs make their debut.

BEST These high-style ovens have it all—sleek stainless steel exteriors, true convection cooking, and larger, 36-inch openings. Menu-driven controls that prompt users through the cooking process make it easier to use convection settings as well as advanced features like drying and bread proofing. Special settings allow programming and saving favorite recipes that can later be recalled. Some models are equipped with speed-cook settings that utilize multiple heating methods to cut conventional cooking time by as much as 50 percent.

Broiled foods turn out more evenly seared. Cooking capacity increases, too. Because convection delivers even temperature throughout the oven, an oven with four rack positions can bake four trays of cookies at one time. Of course, that probably entails buying two extra wire racks from the ovenmaker, but the cookie hounds in the house will surely appreciate it.

Not all convection is created equally, however, and separating convection-lite from true convection is up to the consumer. Convection-lite models just put a fan in the rear panel of the oven. True convection puts an additional heating element around the fan. This method is considered ideal because the placement of the heating element at the back of the oven allows warm air to circulate without creating hot spots.

Most recipes must be adapted to the quick-cooking of convection ovens, either through a decrease in temperature or cooking time. Newer models have an automatic conversion feature that eliminates guesswork, but manufacturers should be able to provide guidelines.

For those who have inherited convection ovens, here's an extraordinarily handy rule of thumb: In general, to convert from standard oven to convection, keep the temperature the same and reduce the time by 25 percent. Or, keep the time the same and reduce the temperature by 25°F. (Do not do both.) For recipes with bake times of 15 minutes or less, keep the time the same and reduce the temperature by 25°F. It's that simple, believe it or not.

FINAL CONSIDERATIONS

Over the years, some advances will come and go, but certain features are always worth shopping for. For ease of maintenance, self-cleaning ovens are unbeatable. (The self-cleaning mode seals the oven cavity, jacks the heat way up, burns everything off the walls of the oven and brushes it away.) Note, also, that dark interiors retain heat better than light ones. Racks should be easy to maneuver yet secure when they're in place. The lightbulb should be easy to get to. Also, the bulb should be bright enough and the opening in the door large enough so that a person doesn't have to open the door to see what's baking. An oven that meets all these requirements is a keeper.

Kitchen Sinks

THOUGH A KITCHEN SINK may seem to be a straightforward purchase, designers call sinks the workhorses of the kitchen. Sinks factor into the entire cooking process, from preparation to cleanup, and this role means proper selection and placement are among the vital decisions in a kitchen remodel.

Points to consider when selecting a sink include size, shape, material and mounting method. Here's how to select the right sink.

THE RIGHT FIT

Standard-size kitchen sinks, with one bowl for washing and one bowl for rinsing, measure 33x22 inches. One size does not fit all, however. Counter space can dictate how large a sink can be. For example, in a 150-square-foot kitchen, a 25x22-inch single-bowl sink would probably suffice. (Manufacturers' sink sizes generally refer to the inside dimensions of the bowl, not necessarily the perimeter of the unit.)

For years, bowl depth was fairly standard at 8 inches. Today, 10-inch-deep bowls are easy to come by, and shoppers can even find depths up to 12 inches. A good guideline is to try to accommodate the deepest pot in the kitchen.

SHAPELY SOLUTIONS

After size comes the issue of how many bowls: one, two, or three. Each option has its advantages, even though personal preference plays a significant role.

SINGLE BASIN These are perfect choices for small spaces or second sinks. The latest designs can handle large pots. They also come in a variety of round and square shapes, making them perfect for adding visual interest to a counter surface.

DOUBLE BASIN The standard for many kitchens, double-bowl sinks allow for multitasking: cleaning veggies in one bowl, soaking pots in the other. Many designers wouldn't dare design a kitchen without at least one double-bowl sink. Those who have been looking at the same sink since the 1980s may be tickled to know about asymmetrical double-bowl sinks, with one larger basin. This makes the multitasking that easier. (Hint: Do the food prep in the smaller bowl.)

TRIPLE BASIN The triple-bowl sink sings its siren song to the countertop-endowed cooking enthusiast. The usual setup is two deep basins for stacking loads of dirty dishes and a much smaller, shallower bowl for food prep. Some of the pricier three-bowlers are accessorized to the nines with special custom-fit colanders, cutting boards, and drainers.

INSTALLATION OPTIONS

A sink can be installed in one of three ways: self-rimming, undermount, or integral. The choice depends partly on aesthetics and partly on countertop material.

SELF-RIMMING This is the easiest and most common method. A sink (with a rim, naturally) goes into a hole in the countertop. The space between sink and counter is then sealed. This is simple for the installers, but it's neither the most sanitary nor easiest-to-maintain option. Because of the lip, it is impossible to sweep crumbs from the counter directly into the sink. So food could get caught at the rim, eventually forming a nasty grunge.

UNDERMOUNT Popular with solid-surfacing and stone counters, undermounts create a sleek, unbroken line across the basin. For this reason, it has become popular among kitchen designers. It's expensive, though, because the countertop must be precisely measured and cut to fit the size and shape of the sink.

INTEGRAL As the name implies, integral sinks and countertops are of one piece. Before, this meant the sink and countertop were solid surfacing. Today, integral options are available in stainless steel and stone, too—albeit at heftier prices.

MATERIAL MATTERS

Material not only affects the overall look of a kitchen; they also affect price and wearability. Here are the pros and cons of some of the more popular materials.

CAST IRON Made from molten iron shaped in a mold, these sturdy sinks have been a favorite for decades. After the sink is shaped, an enamel coating is then fired on for color, shine and durability. Because it's thick and rigid, cast iron will cut down on the noise of banging pots, it also holds heat longer. On the downside, it's heavy, and although durable, the enamel coating can scratch and discolor over time.

FIRECLAY They consist of a clay base, which is fired at an intense heat to produce a durable, glossy finish. The slick surface is meant to resist scratches and abrasions. Like cast iron, fireclay won't rust or fade, but it can discolor in some circumstances.

SOLID SURFACING Like solid surface counters, these sinks are made from a polyester or acrylic base. They're available in a lot of colors and patterns other materials just can't duplicate. Because the color and pattern run through the entire material, minor burns and scrapes can be sanded out with relative ease. The drawback is cost. These sinks, which can be installed seamlessly with the countertop, can run upward—sometimes way upward—of $500.

STAINLESS STEEL No longer necessarily an inexpensive builder-grade sink, stainless steel is primed to shine in the design spotlight. Today's models are better built out of thicker steel (16- and 18-gauge). Advances in technology have made them corrosion-resistant and less noisy. On the downside, it does scratch, and sinks made from thinner, 21-gauge material can make quite a racket with clanking dishes.

GOOD Plain and simple is the name of the game here. Look for sturdy single-bowl designs made of lesser-grade stainless steel. Self-rimming styles proliferate. More popular undermount and double-bowl designs just begin to make an appearance.

BETTER Step up to a wider range of choices. Look for single- and double-bowl designs made from stainless steel, fireclay, and cast iron. In stainless, higher grades of steel appear, eliminating many of the design pitfalls found on lower-priced sinks. Installation options increase as well, with seamless undermount designs becoming the overwhelming favorite.

BEST These high-style sinks are pleasures to behold. Packed with accessories (from colanders and cutting boards to special dish drainers), they make mundane tasks like washing dishes less of a hassle. Ease of use is not the only consideration here—style plays a role, too. Look for decorative designs and fully integrated sinks that blend with countertops.

Kitchen Counters

BENEATH AMERICA'S DISH RACKS AND TOASTERS lie an array of countertops. These surfaces (or collections of surfaces) have to be rugged and stain-resistant enough to handle the pounding, knifework, and occasional mishaps of everyday cooking. Countertops must also be suitably attractive to fit in with or complement the vertical surfaces in the room. Ceramic, stone, and wood have been food-prep surfaces since ancient times. In the past half century or so, plastics and then metals have vied with the classics for space in America's kitchens. The pros and cons of various countertop materials are presented here.

NATURAL STONE

The quirky individuality of natural stone puts mass-produced anonymity into sharp relief. This is great for those yearning for something genuine and authentic in their homes. Natural stone—primarily granite and marble—is quarried around the world and, believe it or not, comes in a range of natural colors. It's available at tile showrooms or home improvement centers.

Most stone can be used for essentially any surface, but granite tends to be more popular for countertops because of its durability, stain resistance and ease of maintenance. Marble is softer and more porous. In fact, as far as liquid is concerned, a marble countertop is practically a wood countertop. Any spills should be wiped up immediately. Marble's one great advantage is its ability to stay cool, which makes it a favorite of baking enthusiasts. Some bakers will deck out a kitchen in another material and ask for a segment of marble top, often at a lower-than-normal height, just for baking. All stone countertops should be sealed upon installation and then resealed regularly.

Stone countertops are not for clumsy people. Any glass tipped over onto a granite countertop will not be a glass for very long. Then again, granite is natural, and it's quite beautiful.

CONCRETE

Concrete countertops became something of a tasty trend in luxury kitchens around the year 2000. Their main attraction is their look, and to be sure, the look is extraordinary. When treated with stains, pigments, and epoxy coatings, concrete can have the appearance, texture, and feel of quarried stone. It also has the potential to take on a sculptural quality, as it can be molded into exotic shapes. Each handmade countertop will have slight color and texture variations and will take on different looks as it ages. Every concrete countertop is a living, breathing work of art.

Alas, the appearance, the prime benefit of having a concrete countertop, is pretty much the only benefit of having a concrete countertop. Most of the early owners of concrete countertops found that, attractive though they are, the surfaces are not terribly valuable components of a working kitchen. Hairline cracks are routine, as even installers have acknowledged. Much of a concrete countertop's success depends on its installer, but given the fact that cracks remain commonplace in streets and sidewalks, concrete countertops would seem best-suited to those who covet them only for their singular cosmetic glory.

CERAMIC TILE

Unlike stone, ceramic tile is man-made, but like stone, tile's basic ingredients—clay and fire—predate the dawn of humanity. Clay is a cinch to dig up, process, and mold into a variety of tile shapes. Even glaze, a glass compound colored with metal oxides, is rooted in historically essential materials of humankind. Without fire, though, the first two ingredients would be all but worthless as surfaces in modern homes. Super-high heat turns raw clay into exceptionally durable ceramic tile and glaze into both a decorative and protective coating for the porous ceramic surface. In the process, the clay and glaze become irretrievably fused into one material.

This symphony of prehistoric elements now comes in an array of shapes, sizes, and colors. Varied tile styles can add interest and provide different functions in a room. For example, field tiles establish a main color, and accent tiles provide a complement. On a countertop, the edge or backsplash can provide a contrast or a match to the counter surface.

Grout, of course, is a major consideration when shopping for tile. Porous grouts can become a playground for mildew, stains, and odor. With sealed joints (the gaps between tiles) or stain-resistant grouts, however, ceramic tile takes little maintenance beyond regular cleaning with soap and water. The tiles themselves take a damp sponge or nonabrasive cleaner. Grout joints can be tackled with a soft-bristle brush.

COUNTER EDGES

Countertop edge treatments, which can be decorative designs or shapes molded, inset, or overlaid along the front of the countertop, can add a special something to both a countertop and a complete kitchen. Stone, solid surfacing, and laminates all offer unique characteristics in edge treatments.

Whatever the material, the narrow horizontal band that edge treatments create in a room can fool the eye into perceiving a space is larger than it actually is. As a continuous design element around the perimeter of a room, they act as a visual bridge between the wall cabinets and the base units, tying the upper and lower halves of the room together. Finally, edge treatments inject contrast—be it through color or a curving line—into what is often a strong, dominantly monochromatic, rectilinear space.

STONE Shape is the name of the game with stone countertop edges. The simple option is eased edges, where the 90-degree top and bottom corners are rounded off. The bullnose edge, a semicircle, is another big hit on stone countertops. A host of architectural profiles, long popular in cabinets, bookcases, etc, are also available. Dupont, ogee and fillet are but three such profiles that are far easier to explain visually than verbally. Those aiming for traditional motifs might opt to stack architectural profiles to forge a classy look and create the illusion of a thicker countertop, even though only the edge would be packing the extra heft.

SOLID SURFACING Solid surfacing offers almost infinite design and color possibilities. Using fine woodworking tools and liquid solid surfacing, skilled fabricators can carve intricate patterns into solid surfacing, fill in the etching with liquid, then smooth it down after it hardens. The result can be one-of-a-kind artwork in countertop form.

LAMINATES Laminate counters offer an affordable, attractive, and versatile alternative. Several standard edge treatments are available, but the main cosmetic drawback, particularly when it comes to 90-degree bends, bevels, or any treatments that require butting two sheets of laminate together, is the resulting brown seam between the pieces. Manufacturers have addressed the issue, though, with special laminates and edge treatments that significantly hide the seams and give the appearance of a solid counter surface.

WOOD

Somehow, wood is just as comfortable in an old-fashioned, Laura Ingalls Wilder–style house on the prairie as it is in a newfangled, Frank Lloyd Wright Prairie–style house. Yes, sliced trees pull off the rare feat of being both warm and cool, but more important for countertop shoppers, wood offers a forgiving place for slicing and dicing without ruining knives. Many kitchen designs combine a segment of butcher block with countertop runs made of other materials.

Once out of favor because of concerns about bacteria growth, wood, thanks to new research, is now in a better light. It turns out wood is naturally hostile to e. coli, listeria, salmonella and other bacteria when it's clean and dry. Over time, the wood itself will kill virtually all such bacteria. Leave the surface wet, though, and it will foster bacteria growth.

Butcher-block countertops are generally made from hard rock maple or Appalachian red oak, and are available in a variety of thicknesses and patterns. The extra-thick end-grain tops (the ones that look like checkerboards) are the most durable for oft-used areas. Maintenance is fairly simple: soap and water for routine upkeep and a mineral oil rub every other month. Light sanding removes scorch marks or other surface damage. (For edge-grain countertops, treat the surface once a month with a mixture of one part paraffin wax to 10 parts of mineral oil. Apply to all exposed surfaces, then remove the excess with a clean cloth.) Then again, if you want to enjoy a wood counter—and will never subject it to the edge of a knife—a varnished wood countertop is always an option.

STAINLESS STEEL

Given the popularity of commercial-look kitchens, the arrival of stainless steel countertops in homes was just a matter of time. Made of commercial-gauge steel wrapped around a wood core and backed with melamine, stainless steel countertops provide both a sleek, contemporary look and an easy-to-sterilize surface.

Over time, a stainless steel countertop will develop what's known as a butler's finish—a web of scratches that some people like and some people don't. The first scratch in a virgin countertop may break a homeowner's heart, but successive scratches will engender a patina that gives the surface character, a fingerprint of sorts.

SOLID SURFACING AND LAMINATES

Solid surfacing, such as Corian, consists of a plastic (polyester and/or acrylic) with a filler, manufactured in the form of sheets and sinks. As a plastic, solid surfacing is lighter than stone, and because it can be worked with ordinary woodworking tools and shows no seams, it offers a limitless panorama of design options. Solid surfacing is also extremely durable and can be cleaned with soap and water or an ammonia-based cleaner.

So what's not to like? Well, it's plastic. Yes, that fact provides all of its advantages, but it also means solid surfacing is sensitive to high temperatures, unlike stone or ceramic tile, which can withstand the hottest pots. Furthermore, a segment of the remodeling population finds plastic surfaces to be a little...well... plastic. Though some prefer the creative and sometimes whimsical patterns of solid surfacing, others insist nothing beats the subtle, organic richness of genuine stone.

The older plastic option for countertops is laminate, made from a stack of plastic-coated papers pressed together under high heat. Laminates come in a vast array of colors, patterns and finishes. Faux marbles and granites abound in both appearance and texture. Laminates are generally far less expensive than solid surfacing. They should be cleaned with a damp cotton cloth and a mild household cleanser, then rinsed and dried thoroughly. The surface should not be flooded, as water can penetrate the seam and cause the substrate to swell.

Refrigerators

REFRIGERATORS HAVE BECOME INCREASINGLY energy-efficient while piling on such benefits as sleek styling, large capacities, and a host of life-simplifying features. With all the advances, homeowners needn't feel lost or overwhelmed; a little guidance will make everyone savvy shopper in the cold, cold world of refrigeration.

START WITH SIZE

With all the food Americans put into them, it's small wonder refrigerators have started putting on some width. The slimmest freestanding units start at 23 inches, but they top out at 84 inches. Built-in units, by nature, are 24 inches deep, to match countertop depth exactly, but non-built-in refrigerators max out at a hefty 33 inches.

Careful planning, including measuring the space for the refrigerator and charting the installation path from the front door of the kitchen to the refrigerator space, must precede the refrigerator search. That's one of those steps that a lot of people seem to forget.

CONSIDER CONFIGURATIONS

With space taken care of, it's time to consider side-by-side versus stacked. Side-by-side models are ideal for kitchens where space is at a premium, because they don't require as wide of a door swing. Stacked models, also known as top- or bottom-mounts (freezer on top is a top-mount), have wider openings, making for easier storage of pizzas, turkeys, and other large items. Bottom-mount units have grown in popularity in recent years. With the most-used part of the appliance, the refrigerator, at eye level, bottom-mounts are the most ergonomic configuration. They also mitigate the problem of having rock-hard frozen foods crash to the floor.

GOOD Basic white, black, and biscuit rule, in side-by-side and top-mount configurations. Expect wire shelves and basic storage bins. Temperature controls are adjustable, but they won't be electronic or within easy reach. A few models have features like ice and water through the door.

BETTER Improved styling and easy-to-use electronic controls characterize these models. Spill-proof shelves and temperature-regulated storage bins are common. White, black, and biscuit are still the standard finishes, with stainless steel just starting to appear.

BEST These units are equipped with high-tech storage offerings: the smoothest rollout bins and drawers that tilt. Adjustable shelving allows for an interior quick-change without emptying the refrigerator first. Sleek contours and stainless steel finishes are standard.

ULTRA These custom coolers blend seamlessly into kitchen cabinets. Improved insulation and electronics (like separate cooling units for the refrigerator and freezer) make them the most accurate for temperature control and energy savings.

Satellite refrigerators, small refrigerators that fit under a counter, are also finding a niche. One company offers a line of refrigerator and freezer drawers that look like cabinets on the outside. Other companies make undercounter refrigerators, freezers, and icemakers, too.

THINK FEATURES

All refrigerators keep things cold. So they have that in common. What differentiates them, then, are features. Some have separate cooling systems for the refrigerator and freezer, which can save energy in the long run. Such models are few, however, and high-priced. In the more competitive realm are such features as through-the-door water and ice dispensers, still the number one–requested feature and thus the most widely available across all models and brands. Other chestnuts include controlled-humidity bins to keep food fresh longer and adjustable compartments to accommodate tall bottles or short jars. Increasingly popular are elevator shelves, which can be raised and lowered without being cleared off, indoor ice storage, and spillproof shelves. Special temperature settings that chill or thaw items more quickly are also big news.

SETTLE ON STYLE

Being appliances in the early 21st century, refrigerators must contend with the restaurant look. Despite that, the top color is still white, with stainless steel gaining ground despite its premium cost. Fully integrated models, which require custom cabinet panels, will blend in seamlessly with cabinets. As with all such appliances, though, full integration essentially means buying an appliance and then buying a cabinet door to put over it, but it does bestow seamless beauty on a room that the family will live with for a long time.

EXAMINE ENERGY OPTIONS

Energy savings are not to be taken lightly. Refrigerators are major power hogs. Old units can easily account for up to 20 percent of a home's annual energy bill. Choosing the most efficient model, within budget, will not only save energy but in the end will also save cash— as much as $75 a year depending on the make and model.

Issued by the U.S. Department of Energy, yellow EnergyGuide stickers, which must be on every new appliance sold, tell how much electricity each model consumes. The EnergyGuide sticker doesn't mean an appliance is energy-efficient, however. For more energy-aware labels, look for Energy Star. These labels, bestowed by the U.S. Environmental Protection Agency and (again) the Department of Energy, identify appliances that are among the most energy-efficient for their class.

Cabinet Inserts

FOR MOST FAMILIES, kitchens are nerve centers, where moms and dads cook, kids do homework, and guests linger. Reason says, then, that they can be cluttered spaces just begging for intelligent storage. In fact, most design professionals will testify that when homeowners remodel, improving storage is often a major motivation.

Key to overhauling storage is focusing on quality, not quantity—or, more accurately, quantity via quality. That is, smartly placed cabinet shelf and drawer inserts can make the same space larger and, therefore, better. Such inserts can take the form of risers, holders, trays, dividers, and much more.

ORGANIZING ADVICE

Homeowners should take the time to evaluate storage needs in their respective kitchens. Open every drawer and cabinet, and inventory the contents, tossing out items no longer needed. Assess how functional the space is. An item should be in a cabinet or drawer close to where someone would use it. That person should be able to find the item without pulling everything out of the cabinet. Daily items should live near one of the five main work areas: refrigerator, stove, food prep countertop, sink/ cleanup area, and serving area.

RETROFIT OR REDO?

Having evaluated the space's storage needs, consider whether to retrofit (purchase stock pieces and work with existing cabinets) or redo (rip out the existing cabinets and start from scratch). Of the two, retrofitting ready-made storage devices into existing cabinets is the easier and less expensive solution.

The downside of retrofitting is that you shouldn't expect a perfect fit. Although cabinet dimensions are fairly standard (the most popular widths are 18, 24, and 30 inches; the most popular depths are 24 inches

GOOD Look for plastic, plastic-coated wire and stainless steel designs that can be used to retrofit existing cabinets and drawers. Selection is limited to basic shelves, stackers and racks. Though a few items mount permanently, most attach to or hang from a cabinet's existing shelves.

BETTER Available through home centers and kitchen remodeling showrooms, these wood, metal and stainless steel inserts fit specific cabinet lines. Look for designs that create concealed storage for garbage and recycling, or racks that keep pots and pans from shifting inside drawers. All inserts at this level are add-ons and not included in the cabinet base price.

BEST A perfect fit, improved styling and ergonomics are three good reasons to select inserts from this category. Look for sculpted cutlery trays, as well as roll-out ones. Remember: These designs are often proprietary and made to fit only the cabinets of a specific manufacturer—so those uninterested in redoing the entire kitchen should shop carefully.

for base cabinets and 12 inches for wall cabinets), most off-the-shelf storage devices are too small to fit perfectly and leave gaps that are unusable.

With that in mind, if an existing cabinet configuration isn't up to snuff, or if a kitchen cries out for a new look, it's time to bite the bullet and prepare for a redo. The advantage of remodeling, of course, isn't only control over the sizes and types of cabinets but also the dimensions of the devices going inside each unit. It's like going to a tailor for a perfect custom fit. This means getting the precise storage for all the items so meticulously inventoried a few paragraphs ago, with no wasted space. For those who choose the remodeling option, understand that inserts are considered add-ons and aren't included in the base price of the cabinets.

MONEY MATTERS

Kitchen cabinet inserts offer three choices: off-the-rack, designer, and custom. Off-the-rack selections are by far the most economical but the least innovative. These simple plastic and wire racks and baskets can be used to retrofit existing cabinets. It's a slight boost in efficiency, but merely a nibble. Designer systems are available through stock-cabinet companies. Although some pieces come in kits for retrofitting cabinets, homeowners who replace cabinets will truly get the most out of these systems. Finally, custom storage systems, available through high-end design showrooms, will precisely fit cabinet dimensions and make the most of innovative storage solutions.

KEY PIECES

CUTLERY DIVIDERS By separating flatware into designated compartments, these containers help create dynamic drawers. Entry-level models often include sections for knives, forks, and spoons. Look for trays with movable dividers that allow homeowners to create their own compartments. Stackable trays consist of a shorter tray that slides above a full-size one. Such modern marvels are perfect for those with two sets of cutlery.

DRAWER ORGANIZERS As more homeowners make the move from wall cabinets to deep, undercounter drawers, manufacturers continue to develop organizers that enable the drawers to be used for stashing everything from plates to pans. One designer favorite is wire racks similar to those found in dishwashers. There are dividers to hold dinner plates, bowls, and glasses. Another system uses a base with removable pegs that keep stacked dishes, mixing bowls, and other gear from sliding around and crashing into one another when the drawer is opened or closed.

ROLLOUT TRAYS Perfect for pantry-style cabinets, these sliding shelves easily organize canned and dry goods. Because the shelves slide out, finding what's stashed in the back is no sweat. Anyone planning to store tall or bulky items should consider a tray with a high back. This will keep goods from tipping back when you move the tray.

LAZY SUSANS A constant favorite, these revolving shelves make maximum use of corner cabinet space by allowing access to unreachable areas way in the back. Newer lazy Susans have sections that pull out, adjustable shelf heights and tiers; and some maximize capacity by revolving with the cabinet door. (The door folds out and away from the cabinet in blind corner cabinets; in custom models, the fixed door revolves back into the cabinet as a person pushes on one side.)

Kitchen Floors

THE FLOOR IS OFTEN THE LARGEST OPEN EXPANSE of any material in a kitchen. Whether a floor recedes into the background or becomes a focal point, it will have a major impact on a kitchen design. Accordingly, it should be aesthetically pleasing and functional. It should also be one of the first things to consider when planning a remodel.

Given the wear and tear a typical kitchen floor has to endure, durability should be a key consideration. Within every flooring material, some products are more durable than others. Homeowners whose design sensibilities are loftier than their budgets can often approximate the look of higher-end materials with less expensive, yet still durable options.

PRODUCT	PRICE (relative to other materials)	LIFE SPAN	MAINTENANCE
STONE	HIGH	Virtually unlimited	Sealing schedule varies from annually to 15 years, depending on stone type
UNFINISHED SOLID HARDWOOD	MEDIUM	100-plus years if treated with topcoat on a regular basis or refinished as necessary	Static wipes, damp mop
ENGINEERED WOOD	MEDIUM-HIGH	10 to 20 years	Damp mop
TILE	MEDIUM	Virtually unlimited; sealant generally lasts 15 years	Damp mop
LAMINATE FLOORING	LOW	10 to 20 years	Damp mop
VINYL	LOW	10 to 20 years for top-quality materials	Damp mop or manufacturer's recommended cleaner

Note that relative price comparisons are based on materials only. Installation fees vary based on material, location, and type of job, and can equal or exceed the cost of the materials.

STONE Natural stone is beautiful and extremely durable. That said, certain types of stone are better suited for a residential use than others. Those in the know recommend a hard, dense stone, like granite, slate, or certain limestones. These stones will not absorb dust and dirt as easily as others, and are relatively impervious to nicks and scratches. Softer variations of granite or limestone have open-pore structures that allow them to collect dust and dirt. This group of lesser stones will start to show wear and tear and take on a shabby appearance fairly quickly if not cleaned semireligiously.

Some homeowners at the very high end have fallen in love with limestone, particularly when paired with such specialty stones as Brazilian Plum slate. One may wonder, when hearing these homeowners rhapsodize, if they've overlooked function for beauty. They haven't. With the latest chemical sealants, slightly more porous stones can be made fit to endure the daily traffic that a kitchen floor must endure.

Stone prices are affected by a number of factors, including country of origin, where the stone is found within the country, ease of transport, and labor costs. Less expensive stone includes Chinese or Indian slate. At the other end of the scale is Brazilian blue granite.

UNFINISHED SOLID HARDWOOD The denser the wood, the more durable it is. Oak and maple are common choices for a kitchen floor, but there are equally durable exotic woods that can add interest to a design. Brazilian cherry or Machiche are high-density woods with an eco-friendly pedigree. In fact, both woods are nearly three times as dense as oak, and both are certified by the Forest Stewardship Council as having been cut from sustainable-growth forests. Naturally, all this environmental friendliness makes these woods slightly more expensive than oak.

Among all flooring materials, many designers prefer hardwood in the kitchen because it works with both contemporary and traditional designs. Wood is notorious for its visual warmth and resilience. Modern finishes make wood water-resistant, and of course, wood can be refinished if needed.

(Quick definition: Hardwood comes from deciduous trees, like maple, cherry, oak, and walnut; softwood comes from evergreens, like pine.)

ENGINEERED WOOD Made from five thin layers of wood that have been glued together, engineered-wood floors are exceptionally strong. The fact that they're prefinished means no smelly—and not exactly healthy—odors from the finishing process. However, whereas solid hardwood, with a 1/4-inch top layer, can take six refinishings, engineered wood can take only three or four at most, as its top layer is only about 1/8 inch thick. Nevertheless, at a lower price per square foot for the finished product, it can provide significant savings over solid hardwood.

TILE Revered for its durability and low-maintenance qualities, ceramic tile is also among the most beautiful flooring options. For centuries, cultures throughout the world have created endless glaze and tile variations. Today, a combination of decorative tiles is often used in a single room, particularly in a kitchen designed in an eclectic manner. Generally, modern ceramic tiles and grouting materials have taken the issue of staining out of the equation. Prices for ceramic tiles remain low, although quality tiles still cost more.

Those looking for a non-ceramic tile option may want to take a gander at porcelain tiles. These resemble natural stone and offer a similar durability at a lower price. Compared with ceramic tiles, porcelain tiles are generally a little more expensive, although the most expensive ceramic tiles may eclipse them.

LAMINATE FLOORING Laminate flooring is a hard surface consisting of a fiberboard core and melamine "wear layer." Sandwiched in between the top layers of melamine is a photographic image. These surfaces can be very durable but cannot be refinished. They are generally less expensive than both hardwood and engineered wood for this reason and because they do not require significant subfloor preparation. Their cost varies depending on the quality of the overall material and photographic image.

VINYL One of the least expensive and most common treatments for a kitchen floor is sheet vinyl. For durability, look for extra tear-resistant finishes. Colors and patterns that run from the backing up through the wear level of the vinyl sheet are also a fabulous idea because any scratches will be less visible. Both features will add more to the cost of vinyl, which is among the lowest-priced materials available. (That probably accounts for its popularity.)

Backsplashes

ONCE DEEMED PURELY UTILITARIAN, backsplashes have undergone a transformation in recent years: They now make serious design statements. Backsplashes are ideal spots for color, pattern, or texture in a kitchen. Whether you're building a kitchen from scratch or just refreshing a current kitchen, a backsplash offers an opportunity for a little fun. The following information will help homeowners make sure their backsplashes looks terrific and perform up to par.

DESIGN WISE

Backsplashes can go in one or two locations—above the cooktop or the sink, typically—or they can continue all the way around the perimeter of the work space. Limiting the backsplash to only one or two areas turns these spots into focal points. By contrast, a wraparound backsplash creates a sense of continuity.

Another factor is how high up the wall a backsplash reaches. The standard—and minimum—height is 4 inches. Keep in mind, however, that some designers think a 4-inch backsplash cuts off the wall, creating a cluttered look. Also, that horizontal line draws the eye along the wall and makes the ceiling appear lower. A more sophisticated look stretches the backsplash from the countertop all the way up to the cabinets. A popular compromise is a full-height backsplash at the cooktop and sink, with a 4-inch backsplash everywhere else.

Of course, appearance is also a factor. The modern approach is to match the backsplash to its surrounding surfaces. A granite backsplash behind a granite countertop, for example, will look clean and pulled together. A more old-school

The subtle colors and textures of stone tiles bring this wall to life.

Laid in an imaginative pattern, ceramic tile gives this backsplash an Arts and Crafts flavor.

SMART AND STYLISH

Though backsplashes pose an irresistible blank canvas for creative expression, overlooking their practical potential would be a shame. These designs illustrate two takes on the subject. A backsplash can play an unexpected role as a light source (above). More practical for ambience than effective task lighting, the halogen panels cast a warm glow. Fitted out with a surface-mounted storage system and shielded by a piece of glass (below), oft-used kitchen tools are kept within arm's reach. Built-in tiled niches can hold favorite seasonings conveniently close to the cooktop or range.

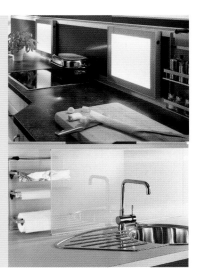

approach would be to create contrast with the backsplash, turning it into a work of art. A mosaic ceramic-tile backsplash or stainless steel in a quilted pattern, just to point out two possible examples, could serve as eye-catching focal points above a butcher-block countertop. Even though the backsplash may seem insignificant compared with elements like cabinets and appliances, it's one of those little details that can make or break the overall look of the space.

MATERIALS

Although the backsplash material needs to be durable, stain resistant, and easy to clean, personal style and that of the kitchen should determine the look. All of the materials listed below are sound choices for backsplashes, but each offers distinctive qualities.

CERAMIC TILE Available in a vast array of styles, sizes, and colors, ceramic tile can create any look or mood one could possibly desire. A common trick is to choose inexpensive field tiles to cover most of the wall and then drop in a few eye-catching accent pieces. When choosing tiles, keep in mind the size of the wall to cover. Ideally, try to cut as few pieces as possible—cut tiles can look shoddy—so pick accordingly. For instance, if the space to tile is 18 inches high, choose 6-inch tiles and set them in three rows.

NATURAL STONE Granite, marble, slate, limestone—natural stone comes in a multitude of varieties and textures and can be used in any style of room. Tumbled marble, for instance, fits in with an old-world look, whereas shiny granite is up-to-the-minute contemporary. Keep in mind that most stone should be sealed periodically to prevent staining. Consult a stone dealer for any special maintenance needs.

ENGINEERED STONE Made mostly of natural quartz, engineered stone is a relatively new product. Colors range from shimmering neutrals to brilliant reds and blues; all feature the luminous quality of quartz. Engineered stone can be installed in slabs to look seamless, or in a grouted tile format. It is impervious to stains and scratches, and requires no maintenance other than simple cleaning.

LAMINATE A tried-and-true classic, plastic laminate is perfect for creating a cost-effective, low-maintenance backsplash. Consider upgrading the typical 4-inch laminate backsplash by capping it with a small ledge; it's a touch that lends the room a more finished appearance.

SOLID SURFACING A kitchen with a solid-surface countertop is a natural candidate for having the same material as a backsplash. The seam between the two planes is essentially invisible, so the look will be sleek and sophisticated. The material can stand up to just about any abuse, and scratches and stains can be buffed out. In fact, the backsplash will wear better because it gets less abuse.

METAL Stainless steel is available, if all those appliances aren't sufficient to sate one's hunger for the restaurant look. Steel will inevitably scratch over time, and other metals may develop an uneven patina unless polished regularly. In metal backsplashes, cutouts for openings like switchplates and electrical outlets are tricky to render and require careful fabricating.

ABOVE: A full-height backsplash, like this solid-surfacing design, provides a more finished look than a standard 4-inch-tall version.

MIDDLE: Engineered stone is more durable and requires less maintenance than its natural counterpart. It comes in neutral to bold colors.

BELOW: Quilted stainless steel panels lend a commercial look.

Wallcoverings

IN SPARSELY FURNISHED KITCHENS, it often falls to wallpaper to be the element that brings dimension and personality to the space. For example, a traditional toile pattern evokes the French countryside; expanses of flowers recall an English cottage; and subtle stripes complement contemporary appliances and fixtures. Although wallcoverings can cost more than paint, their long life span makes them a cost-effective option.

PAPER POINTERS

Of course, the main visual function of wallcoverings is to add interest to the design of a room. Practically speaking, the best wallcoverings in a kitchen are solid sheet vinyl or vinyl-coated paper. They are more resistant to grease and moisture than plain paper or specialty wallcoverings like cork, grasscloth and silk.

Solid sheet vinyl consists of a paper substrate laminated to a decorative surface made from vinyl. It's very durable and classified as scrubbable, meaning it holds up well when a scrub brush is run over its surface 100 times in lab tests. On the downside, however, it comes in fewer decorative patterns and sometimes has a rather drab appearance.

Vinyl-coated paper comes in many more patterns. This alternative is made from a paper substrate on which the decorative surface has been sprayed or coated with an acrylic-type vinyl or polyvinyl chloride. Vinyl-coated papers are usually rated scrubbable or washable—meaning that in the test lab, a sponge with soapy water is run over the surface 50 times without damaging the material or fading the color.

PROBLEMS, SOLUTIONS

Given the fact that kitchens are playgrounds for mold and mildew (for a telltale sign, look for groupings of black dots on walls and ceilings), homeowners might want to consider new kinds of wallpapers that incorporate an antimicrobial protection that inhibits the growth of bacteria, mold, and mildew. That said, most wallcovering failures are typically the result of poor wall preparation. A properly prepared wall also ensures easy removal when it comes time to change the wallcovering. To prepare walls, thoroughly clean them with a non-phosphorus household detergent. Any hint of fungal growth should be scrubbed thoroughly with a solution consisting of 1 quart of chlorine bleach mixed with 3 quarts of warm water. After the surface has dried, apply a wallcovering primer to seal the wall before hanging the paper.

Wallpapers are rated "peelable" or "strippable," reflecting how easy they are to remove. In practical, real-world terms, what these ratings reflect is whether the paper will peel off in big pieces or come off in aggravating little strips.

COST CONSIDERATIONS

In general, comparable rolls of the same quality of the two different types of paper should cost about the same (standard roll size is 36 square feet). Wallcovering costs are affected by quality, durability, color, and design. If the paper is embossed to add texture, that will add another step and more expense to the process. Extras might make a statement, but they'll cost, too: Screen-printed or specialty wallcoverings can triple the per-roll cost.

Other price boosters include sand-dusted or crystal-bided surfaces, use of metallic inks, color-depth application, and intensely colored backgrounds. Dark, color-intense backgrounds are typically more expensive, as they are printed on darker, more costly grounds. Different printing techniques that produce special effects in wallpapers, like blown vinyls and raised inks, will also result in higher-priced papers.

Although cost is always a consideration, so too are design preferences and the use of the room. Wallcoverings in the kitchen are another avenue of expression. Borders can add architectural interest or draw attention to architectural features. Other wallcoverings can add dimension to a room through pattern and texture, rather than just the color of a painted wall. In short, they give a room personality.

SOLID SHEET VINYL

PROS Most durable; best for kitchen and bath
CONS Fewer pattern options; might have industrial look
LIFE SPAN Depends on use; most wallcoverings are replaced every 7 to 10 years

VINYL-COATED PAPER

PROS Fairly durable
CONS Could develop seaming problems
LIFE SPAN Depends on use; most wallcoverings are replaced every 7 to 10 years

PAGES 8–9
Kitchen Encounters
202 Legion Avenue
Annapolis, MD 21401
Phone: (410) 263-4900
www.kitchenencounters.biz

PAGE 11
Lynne Anderson
Linteriors
P.O. Box 1209
Frazer, CO 80442
Phone: (970) 726-1180
www.linteriors.com

PAGE 12
John Kazmir
129 Ontario Street
St. Catherines, ON L2R 5J9
Canada
Phone: (905) 687-7003

PAGE 13
Jennifer Gilmer Kitchen & Bath
6935 Wisconsin Avenue
Chevy Chase, MD 20815
Phone: (301) 657-2500
www.jennifergilmerkitchens.com

PAGE 14
Jim Dove
Canterbury Design Kitchen
Interiors, LLC
103 Ridgedale Avenue
Morristown, NJ 07962
Phone: (973) 539-3339

PAGES 15 AND 17
Susan Oglesby, CKD, CBD
Coventry Kitchens
490 Lancaster Avenue
Frazer, PA 19355
Phone: (610) 644-2773

PAGE 16
Robin Siegerman, CKD
Sieguzi Interior Designs, Inc.
218 Strathallan Wood
Toronto, ON M5N 1T4, Canada
Phone: (416) 785-1341
www.sieguzi.com

PAGES 18–19
Kitchen and Bath Concepts
4702 Mt. Vernon Street
Houston, TX 77006
Phone: (713) 528-5575
www.kitchen-concepts.com

PAGES 20–23
Robin Siegerman, CKD
Sieguzi Interior Designs, Inc.
218 Strathallan Wood
Toronto, ON M5N 1T4, Canada
Phone: (416) 785-1341
www.sieguzi.com

PAGES 24–27
Jennifer Day, CKD
Fairfax Interiors
3739 Pickett Road
Fairfax, VA 22031
Phone: (703) 323-1660
www.fairfaxinteriors.net

PAGES 28–33
Francis Garofoli, CKD
Kitchens by Design
65 Central Street
West Boylston, MA 01583
Phone: (800) 649-0309
www.kitchensbydesign.com

PAGES 36–45
Erica Westeroth, CKD
XTC Design Inc.
39 Marina Avenue

Toronto, ON M8W 1K4
Canada
Phone: (416) 491-9444
www.xtcdesign.com

PAGES 48–49
Jennifer Gilmer Kitchen & Bath
6935 Wisconsin Avenue
Chevy Chase, MD 20815
Phone: (301) 657-2500
www.jennifergilmerkitchens.com

PAGES 50–55
Melissa Smith, CKD
Hermitage Kitchen Design Gallery
531 Lafayette Street
Nashville, TN 37203
Phone: (615) 843-3300
www.hermitagelighting.com

PAGES 56–58
David McFadden & Jennifer McKnight
Past Basket
310 Campbell Street
Geneva, IL 60134
Phone: (630) 208-1011
www.pastbasket.com

PAGES 60–63
Cathy Stathopoulos, CKD
B&G Cabinet
253 Low Street
Newburyport, MA 01950
Phone: (978) 465-6455
www.bgcabinet.com

PAGE 64 BOTTOM
Mark T. White, CKD
Kitchen Encounters
202 Legion Avenue
Annapolis, MD 21401
Phone: (410) 263-4900
www.kitchenencounters.biz